SAFEGUARDING CHILDREN AND VULNERABLE PERSONS IN SOUTHERN AFRICA

Edited by
Mercy SHUMBAMHINI, Isaac MUTELO

SAFEGUARDING CHILDREN AND VULNERABLE PERSONS IN SOUTHERN AFRICA

Preface by
Dr Salisiwe Nkomo

Domuni-Press

2025

THIS BOOK IS PUBLISHED
BY DOMUNI-PRESS
RESEARCH COLLECTION

Law

ISSN: 2999-2508
ISBN: 978-2-36648-240-9
© DOMUNI-PRESS, July 2025

Contents

Acknowledgements.. 9

Preface 11

Notes on Contributors 13

Mercy Shumbamhin and Isaac Mutelo
Introduction to Safeguarding Children and Vulnerable Persons 17

Theresa Sanyatwe
Understanding the Meaning of Child Safeguarding 29

Ncube Mercy
Dealing with Vulnerabilities Encountered by Children with Disabilities 41

Lucia Mutsvedu and Sophia Chirongoma
Safeguarding Children Against Online Violence:
Perspectives from Zimbabwe.. 63

Witness Chikoko
Unsafe Abortion and Substance Misuse among adolescent
street girls of the Harare Central Business District, Zimbabwe 81

Francis Maushe, Etiya Edith Chigondo, Mangwiro and Witness Chikoko
The Dynamics Promoting the Escalation of Street Children
in the Streets of Harare, Zimbabwe, and the Social Work Responses...... 99

Mercy Shumbamhin and Isaac Mutelo
A Chorus of Voices in Safeguarding:
Weaving Children's Stories in Narrative Therapy 121

Michael Bourdillon
Safeguarding Respect and Opportunities: Lessons from
Policies on Children's Work and Child Sexual Abuse. 141

Francis Maushe, Ruth Muregi, Vongai P Mangwiro, Witness Chikoko
Implementation of the Legislations for Child Protection in Africa,
Checks and Balances: A Systematic Review.. 163

7

Acknowledgements

This book would not have been possible without the invaluable contributions and support of numerous individuals and groups. We would like to express our deepest gratitude to the twelve authors and co-authors whose insightful contributions shaped the nine chapters of this book. Their expertise, dedication, and collaborative spirit were instrumental in bringing this work to life. A special note of thanks goes to Professor Michael Bourdillon for his unwavering support and guidance. His wisdom and encouragement were a source of inspiration at every stage. We are immensely grateful to those who assisted with the editing process. Their meticulous attention to detail and commitment to excellence ensured the clarity and coherence of this book. We acknowledge the steadfast support and encouragement of staff and students of Arrupe Jesuit University, as well as religious priests, brothers and sisters. We are grateful to family, friends, and acquaintances for their inspiration, love and encouragement. This book is dedicated to all who work tirelessly to protect and empower children and vulnerable persons, and we hope *Safeguarding Children and Vulnerable Persons in Southern Africa* serves as a meaningful contribution to this crucial cause.

Preface

The safety and well-being of children and vulnerable adults in Zimbabwe face several challenges, with rising reports of abuse, exploitation, and neglect. These issues are compounded by socio-economic difficulties and political instability, necessitating urgent action to protect the most vulnerable members of society. This book serves as a crucial resource, exploring the complexities of child safeguarding within the Zimbabwean context and offering insights into addressing these pressing vulnerabilities. As global attention on safeguarding grows, Zimbabwe stands at the forefront of these efforts, highlighting unique cultural and social dynamics. The exploration of child safeguarding transcends mere protection; it embodies the promotion of children's rights, dignity, and overall well-being.

This book not only examines the specific vulnerabilities encountered by children – including those with disabilities and those affected by online violence – but also emphasizes the need for tailored interventions and inclusive practices. It addresses the harsh realities faced by adolescent street girls, particularly concerning unsafe abortion and substance misuse, highlighting the intersection of gender, poverty, and health. The resilience of these individuals is underscored through effective social work responses, showcasing the potential for positive change. Innovative approaches, such as narrative therapy, are also discussed, emphasizing the importance of listening to children's voices as central to effective safeguarding strategies. Further, the book critiques systemic issues related to child labour and sexual abuse, advocating for a culture that prioritizes respect and opportunity for every child. It reviews existing legislative frameworks, highlighting the necessary checks and balances for effective governance in child protection.

In presenting these themes, the book not only documents the challenges but also celebrates the progress made within Zimbabwe. It aims to inspire policymakers, practitioners, and advocates to enhance safeguarding efforts for children and vulnerable persons across the region. As readers engage with these critical discussions, they are encouraged to reflect deeply on the material, think critically about the shared stories, and consider their role in safeguarding the vulnerable. As we strive towards a future where every child and vulnerable person in Zimbabwe can thrive in safety and dignity, we hope that this book will serve as a timely and valuable contribution to the ongoing efforts to protect the most vulnerable members of our society. It is our collective responsibility to ensure that all individuals, regardless of their age or circumstances, can live free from harm and exploitation. Thank you for joining us on this important journey towards safeguarding children and vulnerable persons in Southern Africa.

Dr Salisiwe Nkomo
Child and Vulnerable Adult Protection Officer
Arrupe Jesuit University, Harare, Zimbabwe

Notes on Contributors

Isaac Mutelo is an Associate Lecturer at Domuni Universitas in Toulouse, France, and a Lecturer and Director of Quality Assurance (including Research, Innovation, and Publication) at Arrupe Jesuit University in Harare, Zimbabwe. He is also a Catholic priest belonging to the Order of Preachers, commonly known as the Dominicans. He holds degrees in Theology, Philosophy, Education, and Law and earned his MA and PhD in Philosophy with a specialization in religion and politics from the University of KwaZulu-Natal in South Africa. Currently, he is pursuing a Master of Laws (LLM) in Human Rights Law and Constitutionalism at Cavendish University Zambia (CUZ). His research areas include religion and politics, human rights law, environmental law, interreligious dialogue (specifically Muslim-Christian relations), and ethics. He is the author of *Muslim Organizations in South Africa: Political Role Post-1948* and the editor of *Human Rights in Southern Africa: Theory and Practice.*

Mercy Shumbamhini is a member of the Roman Catholic Congregatio Jesu and a registered social worker, as well as a member of the Circle of Concerned African Women Theologians. With extensive experience as a spiritual director, narrative therapist, lecturer, writer, researcher, and safeguarding consultant, she has made significant contributions in various roles, including Director of Mary Ward Children's Home and Regional Leader of her congregation. A former President of the Conference of Major Superiors in Zimbabwe (CMRS), she holds both a Doctor of Theology and a Master of Theology (Distinction) from UNISA. Her academic work has led to several publications, a Global Sisters Report award, and service as a UNISA examiner. She has served on several boards and commissions, collaborating widely as a child safeguarding consultant. Her greatest desire is to bring hope and dignity to those on the margins, particularly women and children, with a focus on safeguarding, mental health, and pastoral care. Mercy currently serves as a developmental officer for her congregation and a part-time lecturer at Arrupe Jesuit University in Zimbabwe.

Witness Chikoko is a Senior Lecturer in the Department of Social Work at the University of Zimbabwe. He is also a Research Fellow in the Department of Social Work, University of Johannesburg, South Africa.

He holds a DPhil in Social Studies, a Master of Social Work, a Postgraduate Diploma in Project Planning and Management, and a Bachelor of (Honours) Degree in Social Work, all from the University of Zimbabwe. His research interests include childhood studies, social protection, and disaster management.

Sophia Chirongoma is currently an independent researcher. She is also a Research Fellow at the Research Institute for Theology and Religion (RITR) at the University of South Africa. She is an active member of the Circle of Concerned African Women Theologians. Her research interests and publications focus on the interface between culture, ecology, religion, health, development, and gender justice.

Michael Bourdillon is a professor emeritus of the University of Zimbabwe, Harare, where he spent many years teaching and researching in the Department of Sociology. He studied in the U.K. to the level of a Doctorate in Social Anthropology at the University of Oxford. Arising partly from practical involvement in support of street and working children in Zimbabwe, he learned that for programs to be genuinely helpful to vulnerable children, they should attend to the particular contexts of the children's lives and the children's own perspectives. This area has been the principal focus of his research and many publications over the past three decades. Among his major publications are the co-authored volume *Rights and Wrongs of Children's Work* (Rutgers, 2010) and co-edited volumes of international case studies in *Childhood Poverty* (Palgrave, 2012), *Child Protection in Development* (Routledge, 2013), and *Growing up in Poverty* (Palgrave, 2014).

Theresa Patience Sanyatwe is an assistant safeguarding officer in the Jesuits, Southern Africa Province (SAP). She is also a part-time television presenter of the program titled *SAFE HOUSE* at the Zimbabwe Broadcasting Corporation (ZBC). Theresa is a PhD student at Africa University under the School of Law, where she is pursuing a program in Child Rights and Childhood Studies. She holds dual honors in English and Communication, which she obtained at the Catholic University of Zimbabwe (CUZ), a Master's in English from the University of Zimbabwe (UZ), a Master's in Child Rights and Childhood Studies from Africa University, a Diploma in Safeguarding of Minors from Pontifical Gregorian University in Rome, Italy, and an Executive Certificate in Project Management, Monitoring, and Evaluation from CUZ. Theresa has worked as a child safeguarding officer for eight years and is passionate about promoting children's rights and ensuring that children and vulnerable persons live in environments that are safe for their well-being.

Francis Maushe is a Zimbabwean registered social worker with 13 years of experience in university lecturing, university service, and extension service, and a proven 10 years of experience in programming, monitoring, and evaluation, with special emphasis on program/project evaluation, needs assessment, and baseline studies. He has a solid track record in developing monitoring and evaluation systems, undertaking research, proposal writing, and producing success stories, case studies, best practices, and lessons learned. He possesses excellent communication and leadership skills and can interact effectively with clients, business prospects, and staff. Francis is the current vice chairperson of the Council of Social Workers in Zimbabwe, a social work regulating board. He has served as the chairperson for the education committee for the Council of Social Workers Zimbabwe, a board member for Zvandiri (formerly Africaid), and Chairperson of the Department of Social Work at Bindura University of Science Education. He is currently a temporary full-time lecturer at the University of Zimbabwe.

Lucia Mutsvedu is a teacher, counselor, and child rights advocate. She is currently pursuing a PhD in Educational Psychology at the University of Johannesburg. She is the founder and director of Safety N Us Trust, an organization that seeks to protect children and youth in cyberspace. She is also a pathfinder of cyberbullying and parenting programs in various communities. Her research interests revolve around child protection in the digital space. She holds a Master's in Child Rights and Childhood Studies from Africa University, a BSc in Counseling from the Zimbabwe Open University, and a Diploma in Education from Bondolfi Teachers' College.

Etiya Edith Chigondo is a holder of a Master of Science in Social Work Degree, a Bachelor of Social Work, and a Diploma in Social Work. Chigondo is a senior social work lecturer whose experience in the field of social work spans over 20 years. She has worked in the NGO sector, mainly in safeguarding the health of disadvantaged groups of people, chief among them the Elizabeth Glaser Pediatric AIDS Foundation, AFRICAID, and the National AIDS Council. Social work regulation is also within her bone marrow; she has served in the Council of Social Workers as a board member and at one time as the Acting Registrar. Her research interests include child welfare issues, community health, mental health, social work regulation, and green social work.

Vongai P. Mangwiro is a social work lecturer in Zimbabwe. She holds a PhD in Social Work, a Master's Degree in Social Work, and a Social Work Honors Degree, all from the University of Fort Hare, South Africa. Her research interests include juvenile delinquency, green social work, mental health, gender issues, child welfare, HIV and AIDS, and disability issues, among others. She has seven years of teaching experience in various Zimbabwean universities. She is also continuously involved in various community engagements, including providing social work services to offenders in prison, orphans in children's homes, and conducting awareness and education in schools on sexual reproductive health, abuse, and drug and substance abuse. Over the years, through her academic and professional experiences, she has managed to contribute to the field of social work through work-related research articles.

Ruth Muregi is a holder of a Master of Science in Social Work Degree from the University of Zimbabwe and a Bachelor of Social Work from Bindura University of Science Education. Her research interests are in child welfare and family issues. In terms of work experience, Ruth has been a Research Assistant at Keeptrack Consultancy. She also works as a Project Officer at ADRA Zimbabwe. Ruth has been a Social Work Lecturer at Reformed Church University (2020–2022). She is currently a Social Work Lecturer at Women's University in Africa.

Mercy Ncube is a Lecturer at Zimbabwe Open University and Coordinator of the Disability Studies and Special Needs Education Department at the Masvingo Regional Campus. She is a member of the Zimbabwe Researchers and Writers Association and obtained her degree in Inclusive Education with a specialization in Intellectual Disabilities from the University of South Africa (UNISA). She attained a Master of Science Degree in Special Needs Education from Zimbabwe Open University, a Bachelor's Education Degree in Special Education, and a Diploma in Special Education from the University of Zimbabwe. She also holds a Certificate in Education from the University of Zimbabwe. She has vast experience teaching learners with intellectual and learning disabilities in various contexts. She also served as a lecturer in teacher education for 13 years and acquired leadership skills as Lecturer-in-Charge and was later promoted to Head of the Department (Theory of Education Section). She was also an internal and external examiner in this section. Her areas of research include disability and inclusion in early childhood education, intellectual disabilities, learning disabilities, gender, and human rights.

Introduction to Safeguarding Children and Vulnerable Persons in Southern Africa

Mercy Shumbamhin and Isaac Mutelo

Introduction

The need to safeguard children and vulnerable persons has become one of the most important themes in both religious and secular spheres in Africa. Children and vulnerable persons in Africa often suffer from physical abuse, sexual abuse, psychological or emotional abuse or neglect, etc. In some cases, adequate platforms to lay complaints, grievances or allegations of abuse are absent. In 2019, His Holiness Pope Francis issued an apostolic letter on the protection of minors and vulnerable persons emphasising that "the protection of minors and vulnerable persons is an integral part of the Gospel message that the Church and all its members are called to proclaim throughout the world. Christ himself has entrusted us with the care and protection of the weak and defenceless: 'whoever receives one child such as this in my name receives me' (Mt 18:5)." There have been attempts throughout Africa to create safe environments for children and vulnerable persons, with their interests as a priority. However, several challenges still exist. This introductory chapter provides the general definitions and overview of vulnerable people from global and continental perspectives.

Understanding Vulnerable Children

The protection of children and vulnerable adults through the promotion of practices that uphold their welfare and well-being remains important in Africa. This highlights the importance of putting in place the measures and strategies to protect children and other vulnerable persons from any form of abuse, harm, neglect and exploitation. This involves addressing various religious, social, political, cultural and economic challenges. The No Child Left Behind report by Public Health England (2020) defines 'vulnerable children' as "any children at greater risk of experiencing physical or emotional harm and/or experiencing poor outcomes because of one or more factors in their lives." Vulnerable children are often considered as being at an increased risk of harm based on various aspects such as exposure to violence, cyberbullying, medical or health problems, drug or alcohol issues, disability, family instability, or discrimination based on race, socioeconomic status or gender. According to the International Labour Organization (ILO), Save the Children and UNICEF (2024), globally "1.4 billion children aged 0-15 lack any form of social protection, leaving them vulnerable to disease, poor nutrition and poverty". The lack of access to child benefits often exposes children to vulnerabilities such as malnutrition, inequality, missed education and diseases. The fact that about 333 million children continue to live in sheer poverty and nearly 1 billion children experience multidimensional poverty indicates that the poverty targets stipulated under the Sustainable Development Goals are out of reach (UNICEF, 2024). The National Children's Alliance states at least that one in four girls and one in thirteen boys in the United States are estimated to experience some form of child abuse, one in five children in Europe is estimated to experience sexual violence and 1 billion children globally are estimated to experience sexual violence (National Children's Alliance, 2024). Apart from children experiencing extreme poverty and abuse, those living with disabilities, street situations, those separated from their families and who find themselves as migrants, refugees or asylum seekers also face risks.

Understanding Vulnerable Adults

The understanding of vulnerable children is linked to vulnerable adults, which generally refers to persons above the age of 18 who may be at high risk of harm, exploitation or abuse. (Gunnarsson 2002). The causes of vulnerability in adults include age, illness, physical or mental disabilities or socioeconomic circumstances. In some cases, adults become vulnerable due to cognitive impairment thereby putting them at greater-than-usual risk of domestic or institutional abuse, exploitation or neglect. According to the World Health Organisation (2024), around one in six people who are 60 years and older experienced some form of abuse – physical, psychological, sexual, neglect, and financial – in community settings in 2023. The major challenges vulnerable adults face includes abuse and neglect, financial exploitation, social isolation, limited access to healthcare and discrimination and stigma. Firstly, vulnerable adults are often prone to physical, psychological and emotional abuse and neglect by their children, caregivers or institutions responsible for their care. Secondly, adults with cognitive impairment and limited financial resources may be subject to exploitation in the form of undue influence, scams and fraud. Thirdly, some adults face social isolation and loneliness, thereby contributing to a decline in physical and mental health. Moreover, adults with disabilities or cognitive decline often face discrimination, stigmatization and inadequate medical attention. The consequences of different forms of vulnerabilities include serious physical and mental challenges, cognitive decline, depression, physical injuries and premature mortality.

Safeguarding Children and Vulnerable Adults in Africa

The need to safeguard children and vulnerable adults in Africa remains critical. Millions of children and adults in Africa are exposed to various socio-economic, religious, cultural and political challenges that expose them to risks such as abuse, neglect, exploitation and violence. Safeguarding measures guarantee their rights, well-being and development. Adults and children in Africa continue to face daunting barriers to their well-being including limited access to education, poor health facilities, poverty and unemployment. The challenges also include "poverty, limited access to education and health care, child labour, the HIV/AIDS epidemic, armed conflict, and displacement rank among the continent's threats to healthy child development, as do various forms of psychological and physical violence, sexual abuse and exploitation, and neglect" (Chingwete 2023). The scholarly literature and media reports indicate that many children and adults in Africa face high levels of vulnerabilities including exploitation, domestic abuse and trafficking (Grobbelaar and Jones 2021). Although most African countries have established laws and policies aimed at protecting children and vulnerable adults, enforcement remains a major challenge. Cultural norms and practices have also conflict with safeguarding efforts especially traditional practices that perpetuate violence, abuse and neglect. African cultural practices that might be harmful such as virginity testing and child marriages violate the rights of children:

> In 2018 UNICEF (2018:1) estimated that in Africa 125 million girls and women were married before they were 18, and 30% of women were married before they could legally do so. The absence of financial independence, gender discrimination, inadequate access to education, and poverty are among the factors that contribute to child marriages (Fakomogbon, 2021). For example, in Ghana, where early marriage is frequent, there was a growth of 7.9 per cent from 2014 (19.3%) to 2018 (27%), whilst in 2021 over 80 000 girls aged 12 to 17 were in a

marital union (Ghana Statistical Service, 2022:1-4). Makombe (2016) argues that the debt-bondage practice known as *kuroodza*, in which a household in poverty swaps a girl child with another household in exchange for aid, is a cause of child marriages in Zimbabwe (Tshugulu 2003).

In a context where vulnerable children and adults are at risk of abuse, neglect and exploitation, safeguarding measures help protect them from physical, emotional, psychological or any other form of harm. This reaffirms the need for vulnerable children and adults can exercise their rights to safety, dignity, and protection as outlined in various local, regional and international legal instruments, such as the UN Convention on the Rights of the Child. For the past three decades, African countries have adopted and signed several legislative frameworks meant to safeguard children from various forms of abuse. The African Union has also promulgated several instruments on safeguarding, including the African Charter on The Rights and Welfare of the Child and the Child Safeguarding Guidelines for the African Union Campaigns on Ending Child Marriage and Female Genital Mutilation. The African Charter on the Rights and Welfare of the Child is one of the major legal frameworks that most countries ratified to protect children from abuse. The issue of protecting children from abuse and exploitation is manned around the need to promote their rights to health, education, family life, play, and recreation. The African Union (AU) has also undertaken significant campaigns aimed at ending child marriage, female genital mutilation and other 'harmful practices' in Africa, thereby promoting the rights and wellbeing of children and vulnerable adults. By addressing the root causes of vulnerability, future risks are prevented. Effective safeguarding initiatives and strategies also contribute to the overall health and well-being of vulnerable persons, which are crucial for their development and full realisation of human dignity. From the perspective of social justice, safeguarding helps to reduce inequalities and ensures that victimised and marginalised groups receive the required protection and support.

Breakdown of Chapters

The state of children and vulnerable adults safeguarding in Africa reflects a multifaceted interplay of challenges and opportunities. While progress is being made in some areas, critical gaps are persistent. The primary objective of this book is to explore safeguarding issues concerning children and vulnerable adults in Africa, highlighting the multifaceted nature of abuse they face in the form of physical, sexual, psychological and neglect. A comprehensive analysis of the existing challenges and effective strategies for creating safe environments are considered.

Following this introductory chapter, the second chapter by Theresa Sanyatwe explores the notion of child safeguarding. While acknowledging that the term child safeguarding is fairly new, the chapter notes that there has been a shift from traditional child protection to a more all-encompassing approach. Recent developments have emphasized new ways of safeguarding children which include prevention from all forms of abuse which are physical, emotional, and psychological. This shows that child safeguarding is a concept that surpasses child protection because it aims at prevention which is better than cure. One may question the sudden shift from child protection to child safeguarding. Children in our societies today are suffering different forms of abuse. Most of the child abuses are happening in institutions such as families, schools, churches, hospitals and sports clubs. It is challenging sometimes to identify abuses happening in these institutions, especially in families because of the culture of covering up. The author notes that some of the child abuses are caused by harmful cultural practices which are damaging to the well-being of children. Hence, safeguarding is a call to all the adults in our societies to take care of children so that they can grow up in an environment which is not toxic but which enables them to develop to the fullest and reach their potential. Thus, this chapter discusses what is meant by safeguarding, how it differs from protection, the safeguarding concerns, and how safeguarding can be implemented to ensure the well-being of children.

The third chapter by Mercy Ncube interrogates the significance of safeguarding children with disabilities by examining the different challenges and vulnerabilities they experience in inclusive settings. Strategies to protect this population are also discussed. The chapter notes that the lives of children with disabilities have transitioned from being segregatory to inclusive at all levels, which is a noble move that ensures society perceives them as human beings. This move has ushered in new challenges pertaining to the safety of children with disabilities, especially in the 21st century when children are exposed to numerous challenges and situations that threaten their safety. The safety of children should be prioritized in families, communities, and wherever they go, especially for those who are at great risk. Children who are differently abled or with disabilities need safe environments that support optimal development to be included in society and enable them to enjoy their human rights. These children experience different forms of abuse, exploitation, and violence, which may go unnoticed or unreported because of cultural beliefs and communication obstacles. Abuse and other vulnerabilities against children and young adults with disabilities have devastating consequences, which include unwanted pregnancies, sexually transmitted diseases (STIs), and depression, which impact their development and future lives. Negative attitudes also impact the safety of the differently abled because of stigma and prejudice in society. There is a need to equip the differently abled, their caregivers, and their families with the necessary skills to report and avoid abuse, exploitation, and violence. Additionally, the author notes that legislation in tandem with global views on safeguarding children with disabilities could reduce incidences of abuse and harmful practices towards this population. She proposes a multi-sectoral approach to addressing the safeguarding of children with disabilities in all areas is a necessity.

The fourth chapter by Lucia Mutsvedu and Sophia Chirongoma explores the approaches that can be deployed towards enhancing the safeguarding of children against online violence by analyzing the narratives and perspectives drawn from Zimbabwe. The authors note that the introduction of digital and cyberspace has been a double-edged sword which has brought both progress and ruin in almost equal measure. The virtual world through digital platforms has made children susceptible to a plethora of insecurities which have manifested through trafficking, sexual exploitation, cyberbullying, and direct and indirect violence from their counterparts and adults. Despite numerous efforts, safeguarding of children against online violence is still at its teething stages within Zimbabwe. This has been attributed to gaps in the legislative machine, lack of education and insufficient attempts towards community engagement. Mutsvedu and Chirongoma emphasise the need for laws to strengthen and induct mechanisms to further protect children from various forms of online violence, abuse and exploitation that continue to be perpetrated via several online platforms. This will provide a solid foundation for safeguarding children and deterring potential offenders. Zimbabwe has not sufficiently engaged community stakeholders in developing online protective social environments for children. For this reason, communities need to be mobilized and empowered to detect and eradicate online abuse. This can contribute towards developing a safer and more nurturing digital environment for children, ensuring their rights and well-being are upheld. Despite being handicapped by several disruptions which include poverty, conflict, inadequate infrastructure and limited resources, the country needs to bolster their efforts. To this end, the chapter emphasizes the need for comprehensive approaches encompassing legal frameworks, education, social services, and community engagement. By strengthening legal frameworks, integrating safeguarding education, expanding access to social services, and fostering community engagement, Zimbabwe can make significant strides in reducing the vulnerability of children to online violence.

In the fifth chapter, Witness Chikoko examines the state of unsafe abortion and substance misuse among adolescent street girls in Harare, Zimbabwe. The feminist social work and *Ubuntu* or *Hunhu* (personhood) perspectives are adopted to analyse and understand the realities of these adolescent street girls. The chapter suggests that abuse of substances and unsafe abortion are common among the adolescent street girls of the Harare Central Business District, Zimbabwe. The chapter also establishes the multi-dimensional relationship as some of the street girls used traditional medicines to facilitate unsafe abortion. Conversely, some of the street girls also became addicted to psychoactive substances as a result of traumatic experiences associated with unsafe abortion. The chapter concludes by recommending the Government of Zimbabwe and other duty bearers for the provision of more protection services targeting the adolescent street girls of the Harare Central Business District.

The sixth chapter by Francis Maushe, Etiya Edith Chigondo, Vongai Mangwiro and Witness Chikoko explores the dynamics promoting the escalation of street children in the streets of Harare, Zimbabwe. The chapter notes that street life exposes children to various situations such as sexual abuse, exploitation, violence, child trafficking, as well as drug and substance abuse. Some children die due to diseases and accidents on the streets. The high rate of street children in Harare is a heavy blow to many development indicators as spelt out in the Sustainable Development Goals (SDGs), especially Goal 4 which seeks to ensure inclusive and equitable quality education and promote lifelong learning opportunities for all. The authors propose interventions to address the increase of street children in Harare as well as to safeguard the rights of children who are already on the streets. These include law enforcement, placing street children in places of safety, and making home assessments to protect children who are exposed to harmful home environments. The Department of Social Development, Council of Social Work, National Association of Social Workers, and other stakeholders that have a direct connection with children ought to redefine the role of social work in Zimbabwe primarily in reducing the flocking of children into the streets of Harare.

The seventh chapter by Mercy Shumbamhini and Isaac Mutelo analyses the usefulness of employing children's narratives within their context to facilitate the children's ideas and reinforce their voices in research. Children experience various forms of violence, exploitation, and abuse in Africa and elsewhere in the world. The need to safeguard children has become one of the most important themes in both religious and secular spheres in Africa. With the Convention on the Rights of the Child, the United Nations provided international standards regarding children's rights and societal responsibilities towards them. Article 12, which speaks about children's right to participate in decisions concerning them, is particularly relevant to my argument regarding the inclusion of children's voices in safeguarding issues. Further, section 19 paragraph 1 of the new Zimbabwean Constitution states that "The State must adopt policies and measures to ensure that in matters relating to children, the best interest of the children concerned are Paramount,". The chapter acknowledges the value of listening to children's voices and experiences through qualitative methodology.

The eighth chapter by Michael Bourdillon focuses on concerns that child protection and safeguarding policies solely focused on avoiding specific dangers that they neglect to attend to what children need to develop in their particular social and cultural contexts. A consequence of this neglect is that attempts to protect children sometimes result in damage to the lives of the children targeted for protection. The chapter starts by exploring the case of international child labour policies. Justified horror of situations in which children are abusively exploited through economic labour fuel policies based on an idealised childhood in the minds of well-resourced populations, who are economically and politically powerful in a culture dominated by ideals of individual economic growth. The author argues that the policies obstruct experiences that involve economic activity or travel and that could help children to develop livelihood skills, such as agricultural and entrepreneurial skills, that could help young people improve their lives in precarious economic environments. Such skills are likely to become more urgent as economic systems become ever more strained under the climatic influences of global warming. The international policies can also obstruct opportunities to develop responsibility for themselves, their families, and their communities since they focus on individual rights rather the social interdependence (as in *ubuntu*). The chapter also discusses safeguarding policies against child sexual abuse that sometimes restrict children's physical and social development, by focussing on fear of abuse and paying insufficient attention to the need to develop social integration and responsibility. These strategies often prioritise institutional control and reputation over the interests of growing children. Finally, the chapter offers some remedies on why child protection programmes sometimes fail children in

Africa, which suggest strategies for way forward that serve the best interests of children.

In the ninth and final chapter, Francis Maushe, Ruth Muregi, Vongai Mangwiro and Witness Chikoko offer a comprehensive and systematic review of the implementation of the legislation for child protection in Africa, emphasizing the checks and balances. The chapter is important based on the fact that Africa has the highest rates of child neglect in the world with 41.8% for girls and 39.1% for boys. Sexual violence is reported to be the highest form of abuse from which children in the African continent should be protected. Children's exposure to abuse is highly pervasive in their lives in different ways. The majority of victims of child abuse in Africa mostly experience challenges such as poor physical and mental health outcomes, higher levels of depression, increased exposure to HIV infections and Sexually Transmitted Infections (STIs), and higher rates of unwanted pregnancies. Based on these adverse consequences, child abuse remains a major threat to the achievement of sustainable development goals (SDGs) as well as the socioeconomic development of a country. In the same vein, the increasing rate of child abuse in Africa brings to the fore questions regarding the effectiveness of the existing laws for child protection in Africa. Thus, the chapter also focuses on identifying the effectiveness of the implementation of the existing legislative frameworks in the African continent and identifying the gaps that exist in line with the protection of children using the existing laws. It establishes remedies for the improvement of child protection in Africa. A systematic review was used to review relevant data regarding child protection in Africa through existing legal frameworks. The major challenges to the implementation of child protection laws in Africa include lack of adequate resources, lack of support from the government and other stakeholders, and lack of planning. The major interventions to strengthen the implementation of child protection laws proposed by the chapter include the increase in budget prioritization to strengthen the activities that focus on child protection such as building public awareness through education and encouraging child participation in making key decisions that affect their wellbeing. Finally, the chapter recommends that SADC should set aside a fund that is sponsored by its member states to ensure the strengthening of mechanisms to monitor and supervise the implementation of child protection laws across Africa.

Conclusion

Safeguarding children and vulnerable persons in Africa requires a multifaceted approach that includes legal frameworks, community involvement, and international support. While significant progress has been made, ongoing efforts are essential to ensure that every child and vulnerable person in Africa is protected and can thrive in a safe environment. We hope this book on *Safeguarding Children and Vulnerable Persons in Southern Africa* will serve as a ray of hope and a catalyst for change. By shedding light on the critical issues and challenges faced by children and vulnerable persons, this book aims to inspire action and foster a culture of protection and care.

The impact of this book extends beyond the borders of Southern Africa. It contributes to a global dialogue on safeguarding, offering insights and strategies that can be adapted and implemented in various contexts. By highlighting successful initiatives and identifying areas for improvement, this book provides a roadmap for creating safer environments for all children and vulnerable persons. Safeguarding is not just a responsibility but a moral imperative. It calls for collective action, where every individual, community, and institution plays a role in protecting the most vulnerable among us. This book is a testament to the power of collaboration and the unwavering commitment to ensuring that every child and vulnerable person can live free from fear and harm.

References

CHINGWETE Anyway, 2023. "AD731: Africans See Room to Improve Well-Being of Vulnerable Children." *Afrobarometer.* https://www.afro barometer.org/publication/ad731-africans-see-room-to-improve-well-being-of-vulnerable-children/ (accessed September 10, 2024).

GROBBELAAR Jan and JONES Chris, 2021. *Childhood Vulnerabilities in South Africa: Some Ethical Perspectives.* Stellenbosch: African Sun Media.

GUNNARSSON Evy, 2002. "The Vulnerable Life Course: Poverty and Social Assistance among Middle-Aged and Older Women." *Ageing and Society* 22 (6): 709–28.

NATIONAL CHILDREN'S ALLIANCE, 2024. "National Statistics on Child Abuse." https://www.nationalchildrensalliance.org/media-room/national-statistics-on-child-abuse/ (accessed September 13, 2024).

PUBLIC HEALTH ENGLAND, 2020. "No Child Left Behind: Understanding and Quantifying Vulnerability in Childhood." https://assets.publishing.service.gov.uk/media/5f4f72c68fa8f523f4c3c0ed/Understanding_and_q uantifying_vulnerability_in_childhood.pdf (accessed October 10, 2024).

TSHUGULU Ansley Nonsikelelo et al., 2023. "The Influence of Culture on Child Rights Violations in Zimbabwe: A Case Study." *Social Work/Maatskaplike Werk* 59.

UNITED NATIONS INTERNATIONAL CHILDREN'S EMERGENCY FUND (UNICEF). 2024. "1.4 Billion Children Globally Missing Out on Basic Social Protection, According to Latest Data." https://www.unicef.org/press-relea ses/14-billion-children-globally-missing-out-basic-social-protection-accor ding-latest#:~:text=%E2%80%9CGlobally%2C%20there%20are%20333 %20million,This%20is%20unacceptable (accessed September 10, 2024).

WORLD HEALTH ORGANIZATION (WHO), 2024. "Abuse of Older People." https://www.who.int/news-room/fact-sheets/detail/abuse-of-older-people (accessed October 12, 2024).

Understanding the Meaning
of Child Safeguarding

Theresa Sanyatwe

Introduction

Many times people have heard and they have talked about the terms 'child protection' and 'child protection policy' but fewer people are familiar with these terms. This chapter explores the differences between child protection and child safeguarding and who should be safeguarded, why the paradigm shifts from child protection to child safeguarding. This chapter will also state why safeguarding is important, contextual safeguarding, who is responsible for safeguarding and safeguarding measures needed to create a safe environment for children and young people.

The historical evolution of the notion of child protection and safeguarding before unpacking what safeguarding entails. Child protection became a concern in the societies of the global North in the late 19th century and since then the history of child maltreatment has been well researched and documented. In contrast, the modern history of child safeguarding in the global South began only with the adoption of the United Nations Convention on the Rights and Welfare of the Child (UNCRC) in 1989 and that was followed by the Heads of State in the African countries who came up with the African Charter on the Rights and Welfare of Children (ACRWC) in 1999. States' efforts to meet their UNCRC obligations have given rise to the need to come up with intervention strategies and research in child protection.

However, the first Child Safeguarding Standards were launched in 2002 by a Coalition of Relief and Development Charities that later became known as Keeping Children Safe. In this standard, they state different procedures for safeguarding children. What is safeguarding then and how does it differ from protection? According to Save the Children US, safeguarding is a set of policies, procedures and practices employed to actively prevent abuse or harm on children. Safeguarding is taken as a preventative way of ensuring that children are protected from deliberate or accidental acts that can harm or endanger them. United Nations International Children's Emergency Fund (UNICEF) Ukraine defines child safeguarding as proactive measures taken to limit direct and indirect collateral risks of harm to children. Hence, child safeguarding is identified as any measure taken to enhance the well-being of children and protect them from harm. UNICEF (2023) states that close to 300 Million (3 in 4) children aged 2 to 4 worldwide experience violent discipline by their caregivers regularly; 250 Million (around 6 in 10) are punished by physical means.

Understanding Child Safeguarding

The United Nations Convention on the Rights of the Child (UNCRC) 1989 defines a child as every human being below the age of eighteen years unless under the law applicable to the child, majority is attained earlier (Article 1). African Charter on the Rights and Welfare of the Child (ACRWC), 1999 states that a child means every human being below the age of 18 years. We can notice that most of the countries which are signatories to these treaties/ charters abide by the age of majority as 18 years. Safeguarding refers to the prevention of physical, sexual, and emotional abuse and neglect by anyone who is in direct or indirect contact with children. In this case, anyone can be a perpetrator of child abuse hence, children need safeguarding because in most cases they are less powerful than adults and this makes them integrally more vulnerable. Child safeguarding refers to all measures an institution takes to create safe spaces for all children they come into contact with.

Child safeguarding is a concept that encourages organisations and institutions which accommodate or work with children to set structures which prevent abuses from happening to children under their care. Hence, safeguarding is the responsibility that organisations have to make sure their staff, operations, and programmes do not cause harm to children whom they work with. This means they should not expose children to any situation or place which might cause harm or abuse them. Child safeguarding can also be understood as the action taken to promote the welfare of children and prevent them from being exposed to harm or abuse. Child safeguarding can mean, preventing children from abuse and maltreatment, and preventing harm or abuse to children's health and development. Child safeguarding ensures children grow up with the provisions of safe and effective care provided by either those whom they stay with or spend their time within places of learning or homes. Child safeguarding promotes the full development of children and brings out the best in their lives.

Therefore, the goal of child safeguarding is to create and maintain a safe culture that is child-focused and community-driven through sustained and meaningful engagement with children, their families, communities and representatives. Child safeguarding policies, procedures and code of conduct are the foundation for safe programming standards. Hence, child safeguarding refers to a set of policies, procedures, and practices employed to make any institution safe for children. Child safeguarding is the policies and practices that keep children safe and promote their well-being in all the circumstances of their lives. According to the UNCRC and ACRWC, all children regardless of their age, gender, colour, religion, ability, or race have the right to be safe and feel safe and not to be discriminated against by anyone. This also entails that any institution which works or accommodates children should have safeguarding mechanisms in place to ensure their environments are safe and free of any abuse, neglect and exploitation. Child Protection by Smart Horizons (2022) defines safeguarding as what we do as a society to protect individuals from any form of abuse. Child Safeguarding ensures children grow up with the best life chances and that all individuals are given safe and effective care.

Child Safeguarding focuses mainly on preventive actions to ensure that all children are safe from any form of abuse. Safe Safeguarding Associates for Excellence defines safeguarding as policies and practices that are established to keep children safe and promote their well-being. This includes things such as the safe recruitment of staff who work directly or indirectly with children. This also covers raising awareness among all staff members working with children and service providers on creating safe environments, free from all forms of abuses and on children's rights to prevent any harm occurring to children. Safeguarding can mean, preventing harm to a child's health, development and well-being. It also means to prevent any form of abuse from happening to any child. Safeguarding ensures children grow up with the provision of safe and effective care wherever they are. It enables all children to have the best outcomes in their lives. The best interest of the child is at the heart of safeguarding work.

Every institution whose employees, volunteers and service providers engage directly or indirectly with children has a legal and moral responsibility to care and to do all it can to safeguard children from any abuse or harm. This means it is every organisation's responsibility to create safe environments for children. Now the question is, what is the difference between child safeguarding and child protection?

Child protection is part of the child safeguarding process. It focuses on protecting individual children identified as a victim of certain abuse or at risk of some abuses. In broader ways, child protection is about creating safe spaces or environments for children in the whole world. Child protection refers to actions done to protect specific children from suffering abuse or any harm. Child Protection by Smart Horizons (2022) notes that child protection is very similar to child safeguarding, however, child protection is what we do as a society to protect children who have already experienced abuses such as neglect, sexual exploitation, or have otherwise been harmed. In short terms, child safeguarding is what we do to prevent harm while child protection is how we respond to harm (Child Protection by Smart Horizons, 2022)

Importance of Child Safeguarding

If one picks any newspapers or views online news even watching the news on television one can quickly notice that cases of child abuse are reported left-right-centre which is concerning. We hear cases of fathers sexually abusing their children, mothers psychically assaulting children and strangers killing children for rituals. We also notice that there are many African practices or traditions which are abusive to children. For example, child marriages or forced marriages and female genital mutilation. According to UNICEF, 640 million girls and women living today are married as children, and about 200 million girls and women have been subjected to female genital mutilation (UNICEF 2023).

Child safeguarding is important because it ensures that children's rights and well-being are at the centre of everything we do. Child safeguarding is vital as it prevents any harm to children and allows communities, schools, colleges, churches and other institutions which work with children to intervene before abuse happens. It is also essential because it provides robust evidence which can support legal proceedings in finding survivors of abuse justice. If child safeguarding processes are not in place, children can face serious abuses which can cause long-term implications in their lives.

Another question regards why children need safeguarding. The impacts of abuse on a child's physical, mental, and emotional health can be severe and long-lasting which can destroy completely their well-being and the welfare of that child. Hence, prevention is better than cure. It is better to put measures in place to prevent abuses of children than to react when an abuse has happened already. Unfortunately, violence and abuse against children often remain hidden because of the reluctance of victims to disclose their perpetrators and also they fear to be threatened and to be double victimised. This means that adults should be on watch to help children disclose any abuse that happened to them and also to prevent any harm happen to them.

The Committee on the Rights of the Child (2020) describes child safeguarding concern as any situation or behaviour that places children at risk or has the potential to harm children physically, psychologically, or emotionally or neglect. Similarly, the Nottinghamshire Country Council states that child safeguarding concern is when children are living in circumstances where there is a significant risk of abuse physical, sexual, emotional or neglect. They add that, it can also be where children themselves may pose a risk of serious harm to others or where there are complex needs about disability. Child safeguarding concerns in other words are circumstances which put children at a high risk of being abused. Any abuse such as sexual exploitation, hitting, pinching, bullying, name-calling, neglect, intimidation, cyber abuse and so on, are child safeguarding concerns. These are the situations which need a prompt response so that children are not seriously harmed.

It is the responsibility of everyone to look after children and to prevent any abuse from happening to them. However, sometimes everybody's business becomes nobody's business. Hence, there are some specific agents and professionals who are designated to safeguard children from harm. In most settings, there is at least one person, a team or a committee who has the responsibility to oversee the well-being and safety of the children. For instance, in Zimbabwe, there is a Department of Victim Friendly Unit (Police) who are responsible for implementing the laws which protect children and also taking books on the offenders of child abuse. In schools, some teachers and parents are assigned to deal with safeguarding issues for children or learners to be safe in the places of learning. In communities in Zimbabwe, there are Child Care Workers (CCWs) who are responsible for promoting a culture of safeguarding in communities and receiving cases of child abuse which they refer to the right authorities, for example, to the police.

Child Safeguarding Procedures and Measures

Child safeguarding procedures are detailed guidelines and instructions that support an institution's overarching safeguarding policy statement (NSPCC Learning, 2023). Safeguarding procedures explain the clear steps that your institution intends to take to keep children safe and steps to follow when there are concerns about children's safety or wellbeing. For instance, your institution's child safeguarding procedures should include issues such as, how staff and volunteers should respond to concerns about children and how as an institution make sure to recruit the right personnel to work with children.

Child safeguarding procedures are designed to achieve the following, to prevent any form of abuse and maltreatment or harm from happening to children's health and development. Child Safeguarding measures include the development of effective safeguarding policies, procedures and systems. Safeguarding policies should be well understood by all the people working with children. It should be widely accessible so that all the people working with children can be guided on the safe ways of preventing any abuse from happening to a child or children. The child safeguarding policies, procedures and systems must be regularly reviewed so that they are kept up to date with the signs of the time. Undertaking a child safety review is another example of safeguarding measures. A child safety review is a good way to identify what is already being done in an institution or organisation which helps to expose any potential gaps in safeguarding children and also to establish a baseline against which an organisation or institution can measure future progress. It is important to create opportunities for children to participate and provide feedback. This follows the child's right which encourages children to participate in what concerns them. The researches indicate that children experience safety different from adults. Children are more likely to feel valued and speak up in environments where they are empowered and taken seriously. This is the reason Article 12 of the UNCRC and Article 7 of ACRWC state that every child has the right to express their views and for their views to be considered and taken seriously. Safeguarding procedures also include building child-safe capacity in all the staff members, volunteers and leadership teams of institutions or organisations. All the different categories which have been just stated need to be provided with appropriate training to ensure all the members of the institution or organisation have the knowledge, skills and confidence to develop and implement a child safeguarding framework to ensure relevant legislation and principles are met and respond effectively to any issue that may arise.

Child Safeguarding Policies and Guidelines

A child safeguarding policy provides an institution with a formal approach to managing their duty of care, since it is every institution's responsibility to prevent harm from happening to children they work with or serve. Therefore, any institution that works with or provides services to or for children should have a well-written child safeguarding policy and set of standard operating procedures in place. Every member of staff, volunteers and service providers (direct and indirect stakeholders) should be fully aware of the safeguarding policy and procedures put in place and be subscribed to them. Child safeguarding policy should provide the foundation for an understanding across an institution of its role in keeping safe children in its care. The policy should also provide practical objectives to ensure children are well safeguarded. Safeguarding policy should also provide the foundation for reasons why an institution needs formal standard operating procedures including the safe recruitment and training of relevant personnel, responding to different allegations of child abuse and who is responsible for making sure an institution's environment is safe for all children.

Standard operating procedures are linked to the policy because they clearly state how the policy should be implemented. The safeguarding policy and procedures should be updated and renewed regularly since new forms of abuse emerge daily. Standard operating procedures include risk assessment and risk management in an institution. It also states good practices of safe recruitment, training provision for all stakeholders, project planning and implementation and how a problem can be dealt with. By setting clear standards of conduct, a properly implemented safeguarding policy can reduce the risk of litigation by preventing or reducing the number of situations in which children suffer as a result of an institution's failure to practice its duty of care (Rutgers, 2018).

How are procedures developed? An institution's child safeguarding procedures should clearly state steps which will be taken when safeguarding concerns arise. The Standard operating procedures should assist in ensuring a speedy and effective response to dealing with child abuse. They should be easy to follow and easy to monitor and evaluate. The roles and responsibilities of safeguarding officers can also be clearly stated in the procedures which can help an action to take place.

Contextual Child Safeguarding

Contextual safeguarding was developed by Carlene Firmin and her colleagues at the University of Bedfordshire in 2015. Contextual safeguarding is described as an approach to understanding and responding to children and young people's experiences of significant harm beyond their families. The approach takes into recognition that the different relationships that children or young people form in their neighbourhoods, schools and online can display violence and abuse. Parents and carers have little influence over these contexts and children or young people's experiences of extra-familial abuse can undermine parent-child relationships. This can then compromise safeguard measures which families might have.

The contextual safeguarding approach brings a new dimension to safeguarding minors which is different from the traditional approach to protecting children from harm which focuses on the risk of violence and abuse from inside the family or home, usually from some close relations such as parents, carers, uncles, maids or other trusted adult. This traditional approach does not always address the time that children spend outside the home and the influence of their peers on their development and safety. However, contextual safeguarding recognises the impact of the public or social context on young people's lives and consequently their safety. Contextual safeguarding enlarges the objectives of child safeguarding systems in recognition that children are vulnerable to different forms of abuse in a range of social contexts. Hence, the contextual safeguarding approach provides a framework to advance child protection and safeguarding responses to a range of extra-familial risks that affect the safety and welfare of children (Firmin 2016). Contextual safeguarding seeks to identify and respond to harm and abuse posed to children outside their homes, either caused by adults or their peers. In these scenarios, there is a need for collaboration in creating safe environments for children.

The collaboration should be between the policymakers, social workers, parents, and service providers like those who own different social media platforms such as YouTube, Facebook, Twitter, WhatsApp and so on. These service providers can put systems or controls which help to safeguard children from visiting abusive sites and also from being bullied online by those who send offensive messages to them. Policymakers can create policies which safeguard children in public domains when they are out of their homes. This means it is everybody's responsibility to safeguard children from experiencing any form of abuse within and out of their homes.

Conclusion

Understanding the meaning of safeguarding means understanding all that safeguarding involves. It is more than just knowing its definition. Therefore, this chapter unpacked the core of child safeguarding and how one can practically safeguard children. In a nutshell, safeguarding means all the prevention measures we take or follow to create safe spaces for children and to avoid any harm happening to them. It is everybody's responsibility to safeguard children because children are our present and future. We cannot survive and continue existing as humans if we do not secure and safeguard our children. If you want humanity to vanish just neglect caring for children.

References

ACRWC, African Union. November 29, 1999. "African Charter on Rights and Welfare of the Child." https://au.int/sites/default/files/treaties/36804-treaty-african_charter_on_rights_ welfare_of_the_child.pdf (accessed November 9, 2023).

BARNSLEY SAFEGUARDING CHILDREN PARTNERSHIP, 2020. "Contextual Safeguarding." https://www.barnsley.gov.uk/services/children-families-and-education/safeguarding-families-in-barnsley/safeguarding-children-in-barnsley/for-professionals/contextual-safeguarding/ (accessed November 9, 2023).

BLANE Paul, May 26, 2021. "What Is the Difference Between Safeguarding and Child Protection?" https://cbassociatetraining.co.uk/what-is-the-difference-between-safeguarding-and-child-protection/ (accessed November 9, 2023).

CHILD WISE, 2023. "Safeguarding vs. Child Protection." https://www.childwise.or g.au/page/95/safeguarding-vs.-child-protection (accessed November 9, 2023).

CONNELL Nicole, May 2015. "What Is a Safeguarding Policy Statement." https://nicole_Connell.squcrespace.com (accessed November 7, 2023).

FIRMIN Carlene, 2017. *Abuse Between Young People: A Contextual Account.* Abingdon: Routledge.

———. November 2017. "Contextual Safeguarding Briefing." http://www.beds. ac.uk/ic. https://www.oscb.org.uk/wp-content/uploads/2019/05/Contextual-Safeguarding-Briefing.pdf (accessed November 9, 2023).

———. July 2020. "Academic Insights: Contextual Safeguarding." http://www.jus ticeinspectorates.gov.uk/hmiprobation. https://www.justiceinspectorates.gov. uk/hmiprobation/wp-content/uploads/sites/5/2020/11/Academic-Insights-Cont extual-Safeguarding-CF-Nov-20-for-design.pdf (accessed November 9, 2023).

GUIMARAESE Felipe, 2024. "Research: How to Conduct Secondary Research Efficiently." https://aelaschool.com (accessed April 11, 2024).

———. October 18, 2023. "Writing Safeguarding Policies and Procedures." https://learning.nspcc.org.uk/safeguarding-child-protection/writing-a-safegu arding-policy-statement/ (accessed November 9, 2023).

MURPHY Carole, January 2021. "Info Sheet 93." http://www.cycj.org.uk/. https://www.cycj.org.uk/wp-content/uploads/2021/01/Info-Sheet-93.pdf (accessed November 9, 2023).

NSPCC Learning, October 18, 2023. "Writing a Safeguarding Policy Statement." https://learning.nspcc.org.uk/safeguarding-child-protection/writing-a-safeguarding-policy-statement/#:~:text=What%20is%20a%20 safeguarding%20policy,commitment%20to%20protecting%20all%20childr en (accessed November 9, 2023).

SAVE THE CHILDREN, 2023. "About." https://www.savethechildren.org/ (accessed November 9, 2023).

SAFE SAFEGUARDING ASSOCIATES FOR EXCELLENCE, 2023. "What Is the Difference Between Child Protection and Child Safeguarding?" https://www.safe-ltd.com/what-is-the-difference-between-child-protection-and-child-safeguarding/ (accessed November 9, 2023).

SMART HORIZONS, January 10, 2022. "What Is the Difference Between Child Protection Training and Safeguarding Training?" https://www.childpro tectioncompany.com/child-protection-training/what-is-the-difference-between-child-protection-training-and-safeguarding-training/ (accessed November 9, 2023).

THE CHILDREN'S SOCIETY, 2023. "Child Protection and Safeguarding." https://www.childrenssociety.org.uk/child-protection-and-safeguarding (accessed November 9, 2023).

THE SAFEGUARDING COMPANY, 2023. "Safeguarding Children and Young People." https://www.thesafeguardingcompany.com/safeguarding/faqs/ (accessed November 9, 2023).

UNCRC, November 20, 1989. "Convention on the Rights of the Child." https://www.ohchr.org/Documents/ProfessionalInterest/crc.pdf (accessed November 9, 2023).

UNICEF, 2024. "Violence in the Lives of Children and Adolescents." https://data.unicef.org (accessed April 17, 2024).

UNICEF Ukraine, 2023. "Protection and Safeguarding of Children." https://www.unicef.org/ukraine/en/protection-and-safeguarding-children (accessed November 9, 2023).

UNITED NATIONS HUMAN RIGHTS TREATY BODIES, Committee on the Rights of the Child. December 4, 2020. "Child Safeguarding Procedure." https://www.ohchr.org/sites/default/files/Documents/HRBodies/CRC/crc-child-safeguarding-procedure-2020.pdf (accessed November 9, 2023).

RUTGERS Ed Catherine, May 2018. "What Is Child Safeguarding?" *United Nations Children's Fund (UNICEF)*.

Dealing with Vulnerabilities Encountered by Children with Disabilities

Ncube Mercy

Introduction

Child abuse is a severe worldwide health issue, and children and youth with disabilities are at high risk of abuse (Tsangue 2023:9). Children with disabilities are confronted with challenges and vulnerabilities everywhere, so it is critical to understand and address their specific needs to guarantee that inclusion yields desirable outcomes. This chapter explores the complicated terrain of handling vulnerabilities that children with disabilities face, illuminating the subtleties and intricacies that mold their lives. Cases of abuse are on the increase, and media reports are aflash with heartbreaking incidences of violence against children with disabilities and their typically developing peers. By exploring the multifaceted dimensions of abuse and maltreatment that are encountered by children with disabilities and support mechanisms available to these children we embark on a journey towards creating a safer and inclusive environment for all children.

Understanding children with disabilities

Disability results from the interaction between individuals with a health condition, such as cerebral palsy, Down Syndrome, and depression, with personal and unfavourable environmental factors that include negative attitudes, inaccessible transportation and public buildings, and limited social support (World Health Organisation, 2024). Children with disabilities include those who have long-term physical, mental, intellectual, or sensory impairments, which, in interaction with various barriers, may hinder their full and effective participation in society on an equal basis (Convention on the Rights of Persons with Disabilities 2006). The population includes those with learning disabilities, hearing impairments, visual impairments, intellectual disabilities, autism, and physical disabilities.

Legislative Structures and Safeguarding

Current practices for safeguarding children are rooted in the United Nations Convention on the Rights of the Child (UNCRC), which is an international instrument that mandates states to protect children from any harm, exploitation, and abuse and observe children's rights. Section 19 articulates that children must be protected from violence, abuse, and neglect, 34 encourages protection of children from sexual exploitation and sexual abuse, including by people forcing children to have sex for money, or making sexual pictures or films of them (Convention on the Rights of the Child). A child is a person under the age of 18 who has the right to grow and develop to their full potential in secure, safe environments that are free from any form of violence, poverty, or exploitation (Defense for Children International Child Protection Policy 2011). Any person under the age of 18 may be incapable of protecting himself or herself and may not even be able to differentiate abusive acts from non-abusive practices. Action based on the best interests of the child is a primary or major concern (UN Convention on the Rights of Persons with Disabilities 2008:16). Children have the right to life, education, health, protection, and to live in safe environments that promote their all-round growth and development. All children are entitled to these rights, including those with disabilities, and states have ratified the CRC and crafted domestic policies that provide guidelines on child protection (Constitution of Zimbabwe 2013). All stakeholders are obliged to observe, respect, and promote children's rights. The African Charter on the Rights and Welfare of the Child (CRC) is a regional instrument for promoting and protecting child rights that was enacted in 1999. The charter served as a supplement to the UN Convention on the Rights of the Child (ACRWC) because African countries were underrepresented in the CRC's drafting process. The African nations believed that a separate agreement was required to address the unique circumstances faced by African children.

The African Committee of Experts on the Rights and Welfare of the Child (ACERWC) was established in July 2001 and was mandated by states to monitor the implementation of the African Charter on the Rights and Welfare of the Child. Its main functions include gathering information, interpreting provisions of the Charter, monitoring its implementation, giving recommendations to governments regarding collaboration with organizations that defend children's rights, considering specific complaints regarding violations of children's rights, investigating measures adopted by States to implement the Charter through missions, and interrogating States as stipulated by Article 45 of the Charter, and selection of the theme for the Day of the African Child, an annual celebration that is held on June 16 every year to honour those slain in South Africa's Soweto uprisings (Child Rights International Network 2018). Additionally, Article 45 of the Charter authorizes the Committee investigations: on matters pertaining to the Charter that are based on claims of child rights abuses and about the actions made by States Parties to carry out the Charter.

Nationally, the safeguarding of children is a critical issue that is also addressed in The Constitution of Zimbabwe (2013). The protection of children is guaranteed in Section 19 (c) the state shall ensure that children are protected from maltreatment, neglect, or any form of abuse and (d) children have access to appropriate education and training. Section 81 defines a child as a boy or girl below the age of 18 and further provides for children's rights which include the protection of children from abuse, Section 81 (1) states that (e) every child has a right: to be protected from economic and sexual exploitation, from child labour, and maltreatment, neglect or any form of abuse; and 81 (2) adds that paramount consideration in every matter concerning the child is the best interests of the child.

Non-governmental organisations also play a role in safeguarding children. Justice for Children (JCT) was established in December 2002 as a Trust and is registered with the Law Society of Zimbabwe, Department of Social Services and the High Court of Zimbabwe provides legal services to orphans and vulnerable children below the age of 18 years. JCT popularized child laws across the nation, which raised awareness and made it clear that this section requires its own set of rules and policies that must be put into place by various justice sector parties leading to the development of a child-friendly system with programs such as the Pre–Trial Diversion System, the Victim Friendly System; it also advocated for the inclusion of a section that speaks specifically to children's rights in the Constitution of Zimbabwe (Justice for Children). Against this backdrop, Justice for Children introduced a Child Protection Policy aimed at standardizing child protection measures within the organisation and communities. Section 2.2.1 stipulates that the JCT board, employees, interns, and volunteers must report all cases of abuse as soon as they occur or become aware of such cases, encourage children's voices and views on issues affecting them, create safe and nurturing environments, treat them with respect and ensure their safety in all its activities.

The National Disability Policy of 2021 is an important document that spells out how exploitation, violence, and abuse of people with disabilities must be addressed. Section 3.6 of the National Disability Policy (2021). states that:

> 3.6.1 Both within and outside homes, persons with disabilities must be protected from all forms of exploitation, violence, and abuse in gender-responsive ways.

> 3.6.2 Traditional healers, religious prophets and contemporary health staff and allied professionals and any other persons that exploit and abuse persons with disabilities under the guise of "curing" disability must be prosecuted.

> 3.6.3 Guidelines for monitoring the practices of traditional healers, religious prophets and contemporary health staff and allied professionals that result in exploitation, violence, and abuse of persons with disabilities must be developed.

> 3.6.4 Age-appropriate, gender and disability-sensitive awareness-raising campaigns on all forms of exploitation, violence and abuse must be undertaken and promoted.

Based on the dictates of this policy, Zimbabwe is committed to ending the violence of children with disabilities.

Risk Factors for Abuse and Maltreatment of Children with Disabilities

The causes of abuse and neglect of children with disabilities are the same as those for all children, but several elements may increase the risk of abuse for children with disabilities (Legano 2021). The vulnerability of children with disabilities to abuse and maltreatment can be attributed to numerous factors, such as societal attitudes, stigma, communication barriers, and dependence on caregivers. The prevalence of child abuse is alarming, and those with disabilities are not spared from devastating practices that have negative consequences for their development and future lives. The safety of these children is compromised because of myths, misunderstandings, negative attitudes and assumptions held by society (Raymond 2010:14). In most societies, children with disabilities are perceived as asexual, so no one would sexually abuse them. As a result, testimonies of abuse by children with disabilities may not be taken seriously compared to those of their peers without disabilities (UNICEF, 2007:19). Myths and stigma contribute to the vulnerability of young people with disabilities because it is believed that people with disabilities are asexual and should thus remain virgins. People with STDs can be cured by having intercourse with one of these children (United Nations Population Fund 2018). Both men and women sexually abuse children with disabilities, but no one would want to be associated with those with disabilities because of cultural beliefs. In a study that was conducted in Sweden, a representative from a non-governmental organization reported that people think that no one would want to have sex with someone with a disability, so nothing can happen to them (FRA 2015).

Violence against children with disabilities begins on the day they are born because of societal beliefs. Society attributes the birth of a child with a disability to punishment, wrongs that were committed by one of the parents or a curse from God, witchcraft or failure to appease the ancestral spirits or an avenging spirit of someone who was killed by any member of the clan. These cultural beliefs about disability result in violence and maltreatment of those born with disabilities to the extent of termination of the life of children born with disabilities in some countries. For instance, children with albinism are particularly targeted for ritual killings (Office of the United Nations High Commissioner for Human Rights 2022). In rural areas of West African countries such as Guinea, Niger, Sierra Leone, and Togo children who are born with impairments are killed (Njelesani 2017). People with albinism are hunted because their body parts can be used for medicinal purposes. The UN, claims that people with albinism are frequently killed and their bodies can be transacted for $75,000 and a limb for about $15,000, hence their lives are in danger since their families provide people access to those with albinism. Children who are blind or suffer from polio are branded as 'devils' in certain communities in Sierra Leone (Tesemma and Coetzee 2019).

Being different from others exposes children with disabilities to all forms of abuse. Society may not appreciate the differences among individuals and tend to be sceptical and ill-treat those who are different. Children are simply abused because they have a disability. In West Africa they are considered as a 'half person' hence they are teased, bullied, denied access to food, and receive physical punishment (Njelesani 2018).

They are also more susceptible to abuse due to communication difficulties in speaking out about any wrong perpetrated against them. Those with hearing impairment in Sekhukhune District were sexually abused mostly because of communication challenges they could narrate their stories (Makwela). Individuals who suffer from severe disabilities that impact their ability to think and reason, see and hear, speak and understand, move around, and be physically strong are more vulnerable than individuals who have mild or no disabilities (Marge 2003:1). The more severe the disability, the higher the degree of vulnerability to abuse. Some of these children lack the physical capacity and stamina to defend themselves and escape from abusers. Additionally, children who struggle with speech, have an intellectual handicap or are physically dependent (particularly those residing in institutions) are especially vulnerable (Brandstetter 2014). Children with disabilities are not able to physically defend or protect themselves (United Nations Population Fund, 2018).

Most cases of violence against children with disabilities are unreported due to numerous reasons that inaccessibility services may be unreachable because of mobility problems, stigma and stereotypes associated with disability in African societies. Lack of knowledge to differentiate between assistance and abuse contributes to the failure of these children to react accordingly because they are dependent on significant others. They do not know when a touch is abusive or not. Children with disabilities are four times more at risk of experiencing violence than their non-disabled peers because of how care is provided, the effects of impairment, and the scarcity of programs that support children, their families, and organizations (Australian Institute of Family Studies). Some of these children may require assistance in performing daily tasks that may include bathing, dressing, and other self-care needs. Depending on others for support exposes them to numerous kinds of abuse. Some of these children depend on therapy and experience pain related to disability. In these circumstances, giving children injections or manipulation as part of their therapy could cause them to lose the ability to distinguish between suitable and improper pain (Legano 2021).

Sexuality education is considered a taboo in most African cultures, it is a topic that is not openly discussed with children. Sex education for children with disabilities is not a priority since they are viewed as asexual (Raymond 2010). Perceptions that people with disabilities are asexual lead to exclusion from relevant information that is essential to enable them to know when they are being abused and take the necessary steps to defend or report such incidences. Additionally, children with disabilities are not included in violence prevention awareness campaigns or educational programs, and they lack the self-advocacy and risk recognition skills necessary to identify dangerous circumstances (FRA 2015:57).

All forms of abuse and violence against children with disabilities can occur in their families. Dealing with a child with a disability may have a heavy impact on the family's resources and social life, consequently leading to the maltreatment of individuals with disabilities. For instance, a child with cerebral palsy may require regular visits to hospitals for rehabilitation services. The unavailability of such services at local clinics weighs heavily on the financial resources, causing stress on the parents, which may be transferred to the child. Having a child with a disability can increase stress and lead to rejection and violence for families that are impoverished and lack access to basic support services or social protection. This is especially true if the child is physically dependent on others for daily activities or has a diminished ability to recognize danger or defend themselves (UNICEF, 2022:33)

They can experience neglect and psychological abuse due to pressure on parents, a lack of financial resources, emotional problems, and the unavailability of support services. Factors that make children with disabilities at risk of violence and abuse include segregated settings, children with disabilities being alone with an adult, closed and locked settings, organizational culture, and attitudes such as those that support a culture of closed community and poor leadership and organizational governance (Llewellyn). For many reasons, parents', or caregivers' capacity to manage a child with a disability may be hampered; for instance, they can find themselves alone in a society that does not comprehend the disability of their child; additionally, they might not have the information or the necessary social and financial support to be able to give their children the care and support they need (UNICEF, 2007:17).

Abuse of children with disabilities takes place everywhere. According to the United Nations Population Fund (2018), a study of children with disabilities in Uganda found that schools were the main places where they experienced violence, often at the hands of school staff and their peers without disabilities. Yet other studies have found that girls and young women with disabilities are at greater risk of sexual violence when out of school. Neighbours and family members who know that they are alone can use the opportunity to sexually abuse them with little risk of being caught or punished. There are instances in communities where elderly men and women have sexual relationships with children with disabilities, and such cases go unreported because the perpetrators target these children. Regardless of the increased risk of abuse, the abuse of children with disabilities is frequently undetected and under-reported, which allows the abusers to continue abusing the children (Tsangue 2028). Nobody would think that someone might find someone with a disability attractive on a sexual level, even in examples like these that are published. Additionally, domestic labour, which is the largest employment category for girls under 16 years, is a high-risk environment for girls with and without disabilities because it exposes all girls to the risk of physical, psychological, and sexual violence perpetrated by their employers. The risk for girls with disabilities increases when they are unable to hear, understand, or follow instructions quickly (The World Bank, 2019:7). Perceptions of abuse among Africans contribute to a lack of reports. In West Africa abuse of children is frequently justified as a kind of punishment and seen as an internal family issue that is resolved inside the family or community without the need for outside assistance from the social or legal systems (Pinheiro 2006).

The Incidence of Abuse in Children with Disabilities

Violence against children is a tropical issue that cuts across all children regardless of colour, gender, or race. Children and young adults with disabilities experience many forms of violence ranging from physical, emotional, sexual, and neglect abuse at home, school, and in communities (Makwela 2018). Researchers, writers, reporters, photographers, and filmmakers continue to unveil the conditions of abuse and neglect of people with disabilities in the United States (Crowley 2016). A report in the Herald notes that children with disabilities are hidden away, and abandoned in institutions with poverty, ignorance, superstition, culture, and prejudice, combining to deny humane treatment of children with disabilities and legitimize a range of horrific rights abuse (Rambiyawo 2024). Almost all the young people questioned in the African Child Policy Forum research on violence against children with disabilities had experienced sexual abuse at least once, and most of them had experienced it more than once. According to studies the most vulnerable children to violence are those who are blind, deaf, autistic, or have psychosocial or intellectual disabilities as they are five times more likely to experience bullying and maltreatment than others (UNFPA 2018). Even though both children with and without disabilities are very high in Uganda, girls with disabilities are slightly more physical (99.1% vs 94.6%, $p = 0.010$) and considerably more sexual violence (23.6% vs 12.3%, $p = 0.002$) than non-disabled girls; but levels of abuse among boys with disabilities and their non-non-disabled counterparts are not statistically different (Devries).

Indicators of Abuse or Violence in Children with Disabilities.

Children and adolescents with disabilities are often victims of discrimination and abuse of all kinds, preventing them from fully enjoying their rights (Andriambala 2022). If disclosure is lacking and behavioural indicators indicative of emotional distress are not exhibited in a way that would suggest the occurrence of abuse, it is crucial to contrast the child's current symptoms with their prior functionality, and if possible (and with consent), a thorough medical history from the young person, their parents, and the teacher should be collected (Allington-Smith et al 2018).

Sexual Abuse

Any sexual action with a child, including fondling, sex, being exploited through prostitution or pornography, being exposed to adult sexual activity, or exhibitionism, is considered sexual abuse (Mathews and Collin-Vezi 2017). A mother reported how her child with a disability was abused; the girl would spend her days alone, often playing alone. Her neighbours respected her, but her parents were busy with daily needs, leaving her vulnerable. She was raped twice, once as a child and on another occasion. The second incident led to her pregnancy with an unknown man who took advantage of her condition (UNICEF, 2022:33).

Physical Abuse

Physical abuse includes any physically harmful action directed against the child that can be referred to as any inflicted injury, including bruises, burns, head injuries, fractures, and abdominal injuries or poisoning (Mullberry). This involves the intentional use of force against a child that results in physical injury, impairment, or endangerment. It can include hitting, kicking, shaking, burning, or any other form of physical harm.

Emotional Abuse

Also known as psychological abuse, emotional abuse involves behaviours that undermine a child's emotional well-being and self-worth. This can include constant criticism, threats, rejection, and withholding of love and support (Morin, 2022). Numerous ways of emotional abuse include gaslighting, silent treatment, withholding affection, frequent threats, vicious name-calling, intimidation, threatening to destroy a spouse, and isolating the victim from friends and family (Plumptre 2021). Emotional abuse may be very difficult to detect, but developmentally inappropriate behaviour, such as acting very immature or too mature for their age, can be a sign of abuse, as can dramatic behavioural changes. For instance, a youngster who was confident before and did not require additional attention may suddenly need to attach to adults who are not abusive. Children with disabilities may also be called names, given awful looks and honked in communities and schools (Olivine 2023).

Neglect

Neglect occurs when parents or guardians fail to fulfill their obligations to provide for the child's needs, which also include failure to provide food, shelter, clothes, supervision, and ensure that the child accesses education, as well as ignoring the emotional needs of the child (Olivine, 2023; Makwela and Smit 2022). Children with disabilities in boarding schools are neglected by their families who send them to school in incomplete uniforms, dirty and ragged and some are deprived of access to medical care, including not getting regular checkups and vaccinations (Makwela and Smit 2022).

Child exploitation

This type of abuse entails the damaging or immoral use of a child for work or services. Child labour, human trafficking, and criminal activity are a few examples. Technology has also ushered in a new form of abuse known as online abuse. With the rise of technology, children are increasingly vulnerable to online abuse such as cyberbullying, grooming by predators, exposure to inappropriate content, and exploitation through social media platforms. Children with disabilities can be exonerated from technology-based abuse due to the fact such resources may be inaccessible to this population.

Effects of Abuse on Children with Disabilities

Abuse of any form has adverse effects on all children. It has a devastating impact on their development, socially, emotionally, physically, and cognitively. Abuse can cause long-lasting physical, psychological, or both kinds of scars. The devastating consequences of child abuse include unwanted pregnancies and STIs, which affect development (Tsangue 2023:79). This may be discovered when the child complains about health problems and is taken to the hospital for treatment. Procedures to report abuse cases are followed, but no one would believe the story because of societal attitudes towards people with disabilities. In

Cameroon, Ethiopia, Senegal, Uganda, and Zambia more than half of those who had experienced physical violence reported having broken bones or teeth, bleeding, or bruises according to a 2010 study published by the African Child Policy Forum. Nearly 1,000 young people with disabilities between the ages of 18 and 24. Two per cent had suffered abuse to the point of lifelong disability. In Cameroon, 30% of people reported being forced into prostitution, and over one in three reported having been compelled to engage in sexual intercourse (UNFPA, 2018).

Exposure to violence at an early age can impair brain development and damage other parts of the nervous system, as well as the endocrine, circulatory, musculoskeletal, reproductive, respiratory, and immune systems, with lifelong consequences. Strong evidence shows that violence in childhood increases the risks of injury; HIV and other sexually transmitted infections; mental health problems; delayed cognitive development; reproductive health problems including early pregnancy; and communicable and non-communicable diseases (WHO 2020).

Childhood maltreatment can result in a variety of symptoms and disorders, such as post-traumatic stress disorder, but it can be challenging to diagnose in early childhood and even more so in children with disabilities because of the possibility that their responses to maltreatment will vary from the specified assessment criteria (Brandstetter 2014). Children with disabilities suffer psychologically because of unfair treatment and abuse. Abuse and violence against children with disabilities in school have adverse effects on their education and may lead them to drop out of school and fail to contribute to society (Leonard Cheshire 2022). Bullying for a child with a disability is a traumatic experience (UNESCO 2021).

Protecting Children with Disabilities: Past, Present, and Future Interventions

Since violence against children is a complex issue with root causes at the individual, intimate relationship, family, community, and societal levels, it needs to be addressed concurrently on multiple fronts. Dealing with violence against children therefore involves implementing measures to:

- Create safe, sustainable, and nurturing family environments, and provide specialized help and support for families at risk of violence.
- Modify unsafe environments through physical changes.

- Reduce risk factors in public spaces (e.g., schools, places where young people gather) to reduce the threat of violence.
- Address gender inequities in relationships, the home, school, the workplace, etc.
- Change the cultural attitudes and practices that support the use of violence.
- Ensure legal frameworks prohibit all forms of violence against children and limit youth access to harmful products, such as alcohol and firearms.
- Provide access to quality response services for children affected by violence.
- eliminate the cultural, social, and economic inequalities that contribute to violence, close the wealth gap, and ensure equitable access to goods, services, and opportunities; and
- Coordinate the actions of the multiple sectors that have a role to play in preventing and responding to violence against children (INSPIRE 2016).

Legislation

Globally, states have employed numerous strategies to address the maltreatment of children with disabilities and enable them to enjoy their human rights. States are urged to enact sensible policies to counteract negative attitudes, discrimination, and harmful behaviours toward people with disabilities, including those based on age and sex, in all spheres of life (United Nations). Effective interventions require a multi-sectorial approach. All stakeholders, including teachers, parents, children, communities, non-governmental organizations, and all government departments, should join hands to plan and implement strategies to ensure safe environments for children with disabilities. Article 16:2 points out that states have been mandated to take appropriate measures to prevent all forms of exploitation, violence, and abuse by ensuring, inter alia, appropriate forms of gender- and age-sensitive assistance and support for persons with disabilities and their families and caregivers, including through the provision of information and education on how to avoid, recognize, and report instances of exploitation, violence, and abuse (United Nations). Legal protection frameworks ought to cover topics like rights to healthcare, education, and anti-discrimination measures. Clear legislation gives a foundation for holding offenders accountable and acts as a deterrent to potential abusers.

African Disability Protocol

The protection of children with disabilities is supported by international and regional treaties that include the Protocol to the African Charter. The protocol was adopted in 2018 as the Disability Protocol to the African Charter on Human and People's Rights addresses disability-related issues from an African perspective. It is the legal foundation upon which African Union member states are obliged to create disability legislation and policies to advance disability rights inside their nations. State parties are encouraged to ensure that no one is left behind, and address issues such as customs, traditional beliefs, discrimination against people with disabilities, harmful practices, and the role of the family, caregivers, and the community. Article 11 mandates state parties to take appropriate measures and provide support to victims of harmful practices and eliminate practices perpetrated against people with disabilities including witchcraft, ritual killings, concealment, or association with omens. Article 28 part (f) encourages state parties to ensure that children with disabilities are protected from all forms of sexual abuse, exploitation, abuse and forced labour whilst (k) protecting children from exploitation, violence and abuse within family, institutions, and other settings (African Union 2018).

Victim Friendly Unit

The Victim Friendly Unit is a component of the Zimbabwe Republic Police that plays a significant role in the battle against child abuse. The department is manned by qualified personnel who are responsible for investigating, arresting offenders, compiling relevant documents, and making necessary referrals (Our Children, Our Future 2020). The unit facilitates reports of abuse at any police station in the country and escorts the victim for medical examination. Whilst this is a commendable effort to ensure that justice is accessible to all citizens, the officers may lack the knowledge and skills to handle cases of abuse involving children with disabilities. There are many obstacles that law enforcement officials may face while reporting and looking into allegations of abuse against children with disabilities. In extreme cases, according to The UN Secretary General's report on Violence against children, charges of violence or rape from individuals with a disability are dismissed by police or judges who are unfamiliar with disability under the presumption that there has been a "misunderstanding" or that people with disabilities are easily confused (Tesemma, 2011). These children can be discouraged from pressing charges since they would not make good witnesses on their behalf. A study that was conducted by the disabled children's Action Group in South Africa, cited in AcPf 2010e revealed that 14 out of 36 cases of abuse of children with disabilities that came to trial were withdrawn. For instance, situations that involve children with hearing impairment may be treated unfairly due to communication obstacles.

Childline

Childline is a licensed non-governmental organisation (NGO) that was established in 1997 by Zimbabwean women known as the Soroptimists. The goal of Childline is to end child abuse and provide a safe environment for all children. They provide a free helpline that is accessible by dialling 116. Members of the community utilize this facility to report any form of abuse that they could have observed. The services may not be accessible to children with disabilities who lack the devices and knowledge to report abuse on their own unless someone reports abuse on their behalf.

Embracing the Ubuntu philosophy

Violence against children with disabilities negates the principles of *ubuntu* African philosophy. Ubuntu is characterized by communality and grounding in communal ways of living such as solidarity, love, respect and compassion for others (Ngubane-Mokiwa, 2018). Respect and care for human dignity are emphasised in this philosophy. In the IsiZulu language of KwaZulu Natal, *Ubuntu* is linked to communal care where men and women work together to provide care to those in need (Chisale 2018). Based on Ubuntu, the African conception of humanity views disability as a shared humanity and believes that any threat to a child with a disability is a threat to all of humanity (Berghs 2017:2). *Ubuntu* is a traditional African ideology that stresses human beings are interdependent and interconnected. Translating it means that a person is considered a human being based on the treatment that he or she receives from others. This perspective emphasizes the value of compassion, community, and the intrinsic worth and dignity of every person. It encourages the treatment of others with dignity and fairness 'a person is a person through other persons' therefore violence against children with disabilities does not reflect humanness. Nicolaides & Shozi (2021) say that respect and inclusion of persons with disabilities are interrelated to Ubuntu, those who act unkindly towards a person with a disability automatically lose *Ubuntu*. Maltreating children with disabilities implies reducing them to objects. Adopting the *Ubuntu* philosophy implies viewing children with disabilities as human beings worth human dignity like any other person.

Multidisciplinary Collaboration

Collaboration among professionals working with children with disabilities may be an effective intervention in reducing abuse. This calls for collaboration between teachers, social workers, healthcare professionals, and law enforcement agencies to guarantee a thorough method of locating, reporting, and handling abuse cases. By working together, these stakeholders can develop comprehensive strategies for preventing abuse, responding to reports of abuse, and supporting the overall well-being of children with disabilities (Kudzai Mwapaura, et al 2002).

Despite the efforts of numerous governments to support inclusive education, which enables these children to live with their families and attend the same schools as their siblings, some children with disabilities are nevertheless institutionalized. To meet the needs of children with disabilities, UNICEF recommends stopping the residential institutionalization of these children and giving their families access to social welfare, health care, and other services (UNICEF, 2013).

Norms and values

Changing adherence to restrictive and harmful gender and social norms and values in our societies can have a profound impact on the protection of children with disabilities (INSPIRE, 2016) These children live in safer environments when society views people with disabilities more positively and shows more acceptance, understanding, and supportive environments. Creating a protective environment for children with disabilities requires addressing pervasive stereotypes and stigmas related to disability by dispelling myths, addressing misconceptions, and highlighting the strengths and skills of those with disabilities (UNFPA. 2018). This is critical because the attitudes of society towards people with disabilities are shaped by cultural beliefs and values (United Nations) Numerous sources of media can be used to dispel myths about disability, change societal perceptions, and create a more supportive culture.

Empowerment of Children with Disabilities

Sexuality education for this population is very critical to reducing incidences of abuse and equipping them with the necessary information and skills to report abuse. Education on sexuality must strike a balance between the unfortunate risk of sexual abuse by others and the natural need for intimacy and pleasure (UNICEF, 2007). Additionally, providing self-advocacy programs that empower children with disabilities and peer support networks for these children can help create a safe and supportive atmosphere in which they feel appreciated and safe (UNICEF, 2007) Education is a crucial instrument for helping children distinguish between abusive speech and touch and to build resistance.

Education and Awareness Campaigns

The abuse of children with disabilities can be decreased with the support of public education and awareness campaigns as well as community-specific initiatives (UNICEF 2022:33). These efforts seek to debunk stereotypes and false beliefs about disabilities, foster compassion and understanding, and stimulate the reporting of abuse. These measures help to avoid abuse by creating a supportive environment. The purpose of these programs is to increase knowledge about the unique vulnerabilities of children with disabilities among caregivers, teachers, healthcare professionals, and members of the public. In addition, they offer direction on identifying indicators of maltreatment, suitable measures for redress, and the establishment of a secure and nurturing atmosphere for these children.

Providing Support Services to Children with Disabilities and their Families

Preventing abuse and violence against children with disabilities requires readily available support services that are adapted to their requirements. This includes readily available hotlines, support groups, and counselling programs that are tailored to particular or unique difficulties (UNICEF 2017). For example, in Zimbabwe, Childline is a free hotline that anybody can use to report incidences of child abuse, but society may not be able to report them due to ignorance about such services. Additionally, providing accessible information about available resources and support networks is crucial to empowering both the children and their caregivers. Home visits can be effectively utilized to provide support to families to curb abuse and maltreatment of children with disabilities by addressing home factors that expose children with disabilities to abuse (UNICEF, 2007). They empower parents and caregivers with the knowledge and skills to identify and address abuse at the family level.

Conclusion

Children with disabilities are an especially vulnerable group in society. They encounter all forms of abuse and violence that may have an impact on their social, emotional, and physical health. Combating abuse of children with disabilities necessitates a multipronged strategy that includes early detection and reporting, caregiver support, accessible resources, public education and awareness campaigns, legal safeguards, and professional teamwork. It is feasible to make the environment safer and lower the incidence of abuse among this vulnerable group of children with disabilities by putting these measures into practice all at once. The importance of a multifaceted strategy incorporating governmental policies, community activities, education systems, and healthcare is emphasized in the chapter's conclusion.

References

AUSTRALIAN INSTITUTE OF FAMILY STUDIES, (n.d.) *Understanding Safeguarding Practices for Children with Disabilities when Engaging with Organizations.*

ALLINGTON-SMITH Pru, BALL Richard and HAYTOR Ruth, 2018. "Management of Sexually Abused Children with Learning Disabilities." https://www.cambridge.org/core/journals/advances-in-psychiatric-treatment/article/management-of-sexually-abused-children-with-learning-disabilities/85F1DC94F769B395EAE92224A85151EB.

BERGHS M., 2017. "Practices and Discourses of Ubuntu: Implications for an African Model of Disability?" *African Journal of Disability* 6 (2).

BRANDSTETTER Friedrich, 2014. "The Other Side: Abuse and Maltreatment of Children and Young People with Disabilities." https://onlinelibrary.wiley.com/doi/full/10.1111/dmcn.12487.

BANNINK MBAZZI Femke, 2022. "Disability and Ubuntu: An African Approach to Inclusive Education." https://www.firah.org/upload/l-appel-a-projets/projets-laureats/2019/apa029/annex-v-literature-review-firah-ubuntu-30nov22.pdf.

BRANDSTETTER Friedrich, 2014. "The Other Side: Abuse and Maltreatment of Children and Young People with Disabilities." *Developmental Medicine & Child Neurology.* https://onlinelibrary.wiley.com/doi/full/10.1111/dmcn.12487. Accessed May 10, 2024.

CHESHIRE Leonard, 2022. *School Violence and Bullying of Children with Disabilities in the Eastern and Southern African Region: A Needs Assessment.* https://www.leonardcheshire.org/sites/default/files/2022-03/Leonard-Cheshire-SVB-report-foreword.pdf.

CHISALE Sinenhlanla S., 2018. "Ubuntu as Care: Deconstructing the Gendered Ubuntu." *Verbum Eccles.* 39 (1). https://scielo.org.za/scielo.php?script=sci_arttext&pid=S2074-77052018000100005.

CHILD RIGHTS INTERNATIONAL NETWORK, 2018. "African Committee of Experts on the Rights and Welfare of the Child." https://archive.crin.org/en/guides/un-international-system/regional-mechanisms/african-committee-experts-rights-and-welfare.html Accessed April 10, 2024.

CONVENTION ON THE RIGHTS OF PERSONS WITH DISABILITIES, 2006. United Nations.

CONVENTION ON THE RIGHTS OF THE CHILD, (n.d.) https://resourcecentre.savethechildren.net/pdf/UNICEF+2019+convention+on+the+rights+of+the+child.pdf. Accessed April 25, 2024.

CROWLEY E. Paula, 2016. *Preventing Abuse and Neglect in the Lives of Children with Disabilities.* Normal: Springer.

DEFENCE FOR CHILDREN INTERNATIONAL (DCI), 2011. *Child Protection Policy.* Harare: DCI.

DEVRIES Karen M., KYEGOMBE Nambusi, ZUURMOND Maria, PARKES Jenny, CHILD Jennifer C., WALAKIRA Eddy J. and NAKER Dipak, "Violence Against

Primary School Children with Disabilities in Uganda: A Cross-Sectional Study."

FRA, 2015. *Violence Against Children with Disabilities: Legislation, Policies, and Programmes in the EU.* Luxemburg.

INSPIRE, 2016. *Seven Strategies for Ending Violence Against Children.* WHO, Luxembourg. https://resourcecentre.savethechildren.net/pdf/inspire-ending-violence-against-children-2016.pdf.

JUSTICE FOR CHILDREN, (n.d.) "Our History." https://www.justiceforchildren. org.zw/who-justice-for-children-is. Accessed March 10, 2024.

LEGANO LORI, M. D., 2021. "Maltreatment of Children with Disabilities." *American Academy of Pediatrics* 147(5). https://publications.aap.org/pediatrics/ article/147/5/e2021050920/180813/Maltreatment-of-Children-With-Disabilities.

MARGE Dorothy K., 2003. *A Call to Action: Ending Crimes of Violence Against Children and Adults with Disabilities: A Report to the Nation.* New York: Sunny Medical University.

MATHEWS Ben and COLLIN-VEZINA Delphine, 2017. "Child Sexual Abuse: Toward a Conceptual Model and Definition." *Trauma, Violence, and Abuse* 20 (2).

MATHEWS M. Makwela and SMIT Elizabeth I., 2022. "Psychosocial Challenges of Children with Disabilities in Sekhukhune District, Limpopo Province of South Africa: Towards a Responsive Integrated Disability Strategy." *African Journal of Disability* 11(0): a799.

MULLBERRY Care. n.d. "Recognizing Abuse and Neglect." https://www.proceduresonline.com/mulberrycare/p_recog_abuse.html.

MWAPAURA, Kudzai, Witness CHIKOKO, Kudzai NYABEZE, Itai KABONGA, and Kwashirai ZVOKUOMBA. 2022. "Provision of Child Protection Services in Zimbabwe: Review of the Human Rights Perspective." https://www.tand fonline.com/doi/full/10.1080/23311886.2022.2136606.

NJELESANI Janet, HASHEMI Goli, CAMERON Cathy, CAMEROON Deb, RICHARD Danielle and PARNEYS Penny, 2018. "From the Day They Are Born: A Qualitative Study Exploring Violence Against Children with Disabilities in West Africa." *BMC Public Health* 18:153.

OFFICE OF THE UNITED NATIONS HIGH COMMISSIONER FOR HUMAN RIGHTS, 2022. *Fact Sheet: Children with Disabilities.* https://www.unicef.org/media/ 128976/file/UNICEF%20Fact%20Sheet%20:%20Children%20with%20Dis abilities.pdf. Accessed April 10, 2024.

PINHEIRO P., 2006. *World Report on Violence Against Children.* UNICEF. https://www.unicef.org/lac/full_tex(3).pdf. Accessed March 1, 2024.

PLUMPTRE Elizabeth, 2021. "Mental Health Effects of Different Types of Abuse." *Verywellmind.* https://www.verywellmind.com/how-does-abuse-affect-men tal-health-5203897.

PROTOCOL TO THE AFRICAN CHARTER ON HUMAN AND PEOPLE'S RIGHTS ON THE RIGHTS OF PEOPLE WITH DISABILITIES IN AFRICA. 2018. https://au.int/sites/de fault/files/treaties/36440-treaty-protocol_to_the_achpr_on_the_rights_of_ persons_with_disabilities_in_africa_e.pdf.

RAMBIYAWO Lovemore, 2024. "Hidden Dimensions of Violence Against People with Disabilities." *Herald.* Harare: Herald House.

RAYMOND A., 2010. *Safeguarding and Protecting Children with Disabilities and Special Educational Needs.* London: Optimus Education eBooks.

SINDILE A. Ngubane-Mokiwa, 2018. "Ubuntu Considered in Light of Exclusion of People with Disabilities." *African Journal of Disability.* http://dx. doi.org/10.4102/ajod.v7i0.460.

TESEMMA Shimelis Tsegaye and COETZEE Susanna Abigaêl, 2019. "Conflicting Discourseson Conceptualising Children with Disabilities in Africa." *African Disability Rights Yearbook* 7:59–80. http://doi.org/10.29053/2413-7138/ 2019/v7a3. Accessed April 10, 2024.

THE CONSTITUTION OF ZIMBABWE, 2013. Harare: Printflow.

THE WORLD BANK, 2019. *Violence Against Women and Girls (VAWG).* http://www.vawgresourcesguide.org.

TSANGUE Glory Tchiaze, CHIRAC AWA Jacque, NSONO Josephine, AYIMA Charlotte W. and TIH Pius M., 2022. "Non-Disclosure of Abuse in Children and Young Adults with Disabilities: Reasons and Mitigation Strategies." *African Journal of Disability.* https://ajod.org/index.php/ajod/article/ view/1025/2112.

TSANGUE Gloria Tchiaze, NSONO Josephine, CHIRAC AWA Jacques, WENZE AYIMA Charlotte and MUFFIN TIN Pius, 2023. "Abuses and Consequences on Children and Young Adults with Disabilities (CYWDS) in the Northwest Region of Cameroon." *Herald Scholarly Open Access, Journal of Physical Medicine, Rehabilitation, and Disabilities* 70 (9), 79.

TSEGAGE TESEMMA Shimelis, 2011. *Educating Children with Disabilities in Africa: Towards a Policy of Inclusion.* Addis Ababa: The African Child Policy Forum (ACPF).

UNESCO, 2009. *International Technical Guidance on Sexuality Education: An Evidence-Informed Approach for Schools, Teachers, and Health Educators.* Volume I. https://unesdoc.unesco.org/ark:/48223/pf0000183281.

UNESCO, 2021. "Bullying Rates Higher for Children with Disabilities." https:/ /www.unesco.org/en/articles/bullying-rates-higher-children-disabilities.

UNICEF, 2007. *Promoting the Rights of Children with Disabilities.* Denmark: Innocenti Research Centre.

UNICEF, 2022. *Fact Sheet: Children with Disabilities.* https://www.unicef.org/ media/128976/file/UNICEF%20Fact%20Sheet%20:%20Children%20with %20Disabilities.pdf.

UNITED NATIONS, 2008. *The UN Convention on the Rights of Persons with Disabilities.* London: Leonard Cheshire Disability.

UNITED NATIONS POPULATION FUND, 2018. "Five Things You Didn't Know About Disability and Sexual Violence." https://www.unfpa.org/news/five-things-you-didnt-know-about-disability-and-sexual-violence.

UNFPA, 2018. *Young Persons with Disabilities: A Global Study on Ending Gender-Based Violence and Realizing Sexual and Reproductive Health and Rights.* https://www.unfpa.org/sites/default/files/pub-pdf/Final_Global_Stu dy_English_3_Oct.pdf.

UNICEF, 2007. *Promoting the Rights of Children with Disabilities.* https://www.un.org/esa/socdev/unyin/documents/children_disability_rights.pdf.

UNICEF, 2013. *The State of the World's Children: Children with Disabilities.* https://www.unicef.org/media/126356/file/SOWC2013-Child-Protection.pdf.

UNICEF, 2022. "Fact Sheet: Children with Disabilities." https://www.unicef.org/media/128976/file/UNICEF%20Fact%20Sheet%20:%20Children%20with%20Disabilities.pdf.

UNITED NATIONS, n.d. *Toolkit on Disability for Africa: Culture, Beliefs, and Disability.* https://www.un.org/esa/socdev/documents/disability/Toolkit/Cul tures-Beliefs-Disability.pdf.

VILLOT Jimena, 2017. "The Stigma of Disabilities in Africa and the Challenges Caused for Children in Education." https://centreforafricanjustice.org/the-sti gma-of-disabilities-in-africa-and-the-challenges-caused-for-children-in-edu cation/. Accessed April 10, 2024.

WHO, 2020. *Global Status Report on Preventing Violence Against Children.* https://iris.who.int/bitstream/handle/10665/332394/9789240004191-eng.pdf ?sequence=1.

WORLD HEALTH ORGANISATION, 2024. "Disability." https://www.who.int/health-topics/disability#tab=tab_1. Accessed January 4, 2024.

Safeguarding Children Against Online Violence: Perspectives from Zimbabwe

Lucia Mutsvedu and Sophia Chirongoma

Introduction and Context

The advent of the cyber age earmarked a paradigm shift in communication, learning and interpersonal interaction. Even so, this advancement in technology brought a plethora of hurdles, which include cyber violence against children. In Zimbabwe, where there has been a rapid rise in internet penetration, the safety and protection of minors from online threats is now an urgent concern. This chapter aims to underscore the mechanisms and approaches that can be deployed to efficiently protect minors from online violence in Zimbabwe.

Zimbabwe is a country situated in the global south within the African continent and from recent survey data, it has been ranked one of the most expensive places to purchase mobile data. This can be attributed to the inadequate presence of internet satellites established throughout the country. The small-scale development of digital hubs within communities as well as the inaccessibility of online reporting portals has made the country a hotspot for children to continue experiencing online exploitation (The African Child Policy Forum, 2014).

Children's exposure to online resources was intensified and perpetuated by the COVID-19 pandemic. The education sector had to adopt remote, virtual and e-learning methods due to the pandemic restrictions enforced by the government and this meant that children's presence and time spent online was augmented. While digital solutions provide huge opportunities for sustaining and promoting children's rights, these same tools may also increase children's exposure to online risks (UNICEF, 2020). According to Child Online Safety (2019), screen addiction and greater susceptibility to cyber violence and internet abuse are the new dangers that most children face. These digital vices are a cause of growing concern. Children in Zimbabwe are increasingly becoming targets of internet abuse, grooming and exploitation, with techno-savvy criminals soliciting these children to perform inappropriate actions that jeopardize their safety, ultimately putting their lives and those of their loved ones in danger (Gonye, 2022). Research conducted in Bulawayo and other provinces such as Matabeleland North and Matabeleland South reveals that 82% of child victims are digitally violated by someone who knows them. What is even more worrisome is the fact that some children have been reported to be using social media platforms such as WhatsApp to recruit fellow classmates into cyberbullying gangs (Simani, 2020).

In Zimbabwe, the majority of cases of cyber violence are not reported because it is difficult for the perpetrators who have committed online violence to be traced. Since most of these acts of cyber violence occur online, it is often challenging for children to recall the exact words or threats of the online perpetrator. Due to under-reporting and in some cases no reports being lodged, prosecution of the perpetrators is usually limited. In addition, the prosecution process for such individuals is not explicitly mentioned in statutory instruments protecting children even in the recent Data Protection Act (Mabvurira and Machimbidza, 2022).

Zimbabwe is catching up on taking multi-level approaches in addressing online violence, especially targeted towards children through government initiatives, media, and private and non-profit organizations by raising public awareness of the negative impacts of online violence on the growth and development of children. Despite the setbacks and the economic hardships facing Zimbabwe, it should be noted that it has made some significant strides in attaining child safeguarding measures both online and offline. Efforts from both the government and private sector have been monumental in spearheading child online safety initiatives (Mabvurira and Machimbidza, 2022). In 2020, a variety of players in the civil society sector came up with a draft of a child online safeguarding policy to mitigate cyber violence. This child online safeguarding policy draft was instrumental in that it spearheaded the development of the cyber-crime bill which was gazetted by the Ministry of Justice and Parliamentary Affairs in conjunction with the Zimbabwe Child Online Protection Committee. The draft contained guidelines for civil society organizations to adhere whenever they interact with children at the workplace.

Several workshops have been held to conscientise members of the civil society, mainly caregivers and foster parents about the types of online violence that predominantly affect children. These are mainly sexual forms of online violence as well as the reporting mechanisms (Mabvurira and Machimbidza, 2022. In 2021, The Zimbabwean Government introduced the Zimbabwean Child Online Protection Task (ZICOP) within the Harare Metropolitan Province whose sole mandate was to launch as many child online safeguarding initiatives at both national and provincial levels (Masenga, 2019). In addition, they ratified the UNCRC Optional Protocol on the Sale of Children, Child Prostitution and Child Pornography as well as enforcing the Data Protection Act [Chapter 11:12].

A number of Zimbabwe's NGOs have executed public communication campaigns to address online violence against children, especially during and after the onset of the COVID-19 pandemic. According to UNICEF (2021), NGOs in Zimbabwe are engaged in activities to help address online violence against children, including some communication interventions directed at parents, educators and communities, and some advocacy to end different types of child abuse. Fegert and Stötzel (2016) however note that the communication campaign constitutes only part of the process of reaching the goal of ending online child abuse and must be integrated with a comprehensive undertaking that includes the execution of adequate policies and regulations, law enforcement, prevention programming, and treatment services. Accordingly, the overall goal is to impact knowledge, attitudes, and practices, and to create a supportive environment for victims of online violence, as well as reaffirming the fact that online violence against children must never be viewed as normal, but as harmful.

In Zimbabwe, children are increasingly vulnerable to numerous manifestations of online violence putting their emotional, mental and physical well-being at risk. Incomprehensive awareness and measures to safeguard children from online threats continuously aggravate the situation. Therefore, it is vital to address this phenomenon by conducting studies that reflect the magnitude of the problem, identifying the tributary factors to vulnerability and proposing meaningful approaches to curb online violence and promote the well-being of children in Zimbabwe.

Ecological Model

In order to safeguard children against online violence, there is a need to tackle the problems and crimes emanating from digital use through multi-sectoral interventions. This chapter adopts the Systems Theory which is an ecological model proposed by the developmental psychologist Bronfenbrenner, 1979. The core concept of an ecological model is that behaviour has multiple levels of influences, often including intrapersonal (biological, psychological), interpersonal (social, cultural), organizational, community, physical environmental and policy. Ecological models are believed to provide comprehensive frameworks for understanding the multiple and interacting determinants of health behaviours (Bronfenbrenner, 1979). More importantly, for this study, the systems theory was used to advance and inform comprehensive intervention methods that scientifically target mechanisms of change at every level of influence. Societal change is expected to be maximized when environments and policies support healthful choices, when social norms and social support for healthful choices are strong, and when individuals are motivated and educated to make those choices. In sync with this theory, the chapter restates the fact that in the 21st century, it is futile for any one sector to attempt to singlehandedly address the challenges that are brought by the digital world and hope to succeed in holistically safeguarding children's safety (Edberg, Shaikh, Rimal, Rassool & Mthembu, 2017). Hence, there is a need for small to large sectors to converge to come up with ways to promote children's safety from online violence.

Safeguarding Children Against Online Violence

In collaboration with *Safety n Us,* one of the leading Non-Governmental Organizations on online safety, in 2022, the first author of this chapter surveyed online safety in Zimbabwe. The survey sought to investigate the levels of online safety awareness within Zimbabwean communities. The survey questionnaire consisted of ten questions which sought to establish the age of respondents, gender, hours spent on social media per day, social media platforms used, level of safety, biggest threat online, number of times a person added a stranger to online social networks, number of times a person met in person with someone he or she first met online, where to report when you feel vulnerable online and the need for information on online safety.

The research results are based on a completed survey of 240 respondents including 160 children and 80 young adults including caregivers, community members, teachers, community leaders and law enforcement officials. 10 interviews were equally split among the respondents in order to corroborate data from the respondents. A semi-structured interview guide which included a set of open-ended questions related to the research objectives to effectively collect qualitative data.

Age

The survey targeted the children and their caregivers from the age of 10 to 40 years of age. According to the Zimbabwean Constitution, a child is anyone below the age of 18, which makes a total of 30% children from the total population. The results show that 30% were children (below 18 years according to the Zimbabwean constitution), 37% were the youth, while 33% were over 35 years of age. Figure 1 below illustrates these statistics.

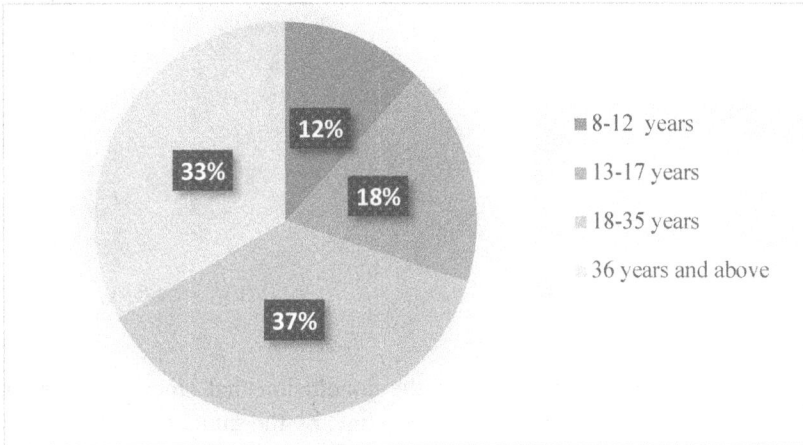

Figure 1. Age of respondents

Most respondents were 18 years old and above. This indicates that, from the age of 18 years going up, they have more access to online platforms as compared to those below the age of 18. Ultimately, it means that technology use has increased in Zimbabwe. Strikingly, 12% of the respondents were below the age of 13, which poses a very big risk to children who are not mature enough to make decisions online and more importantly, most platforms like Facebook, Instagram and Twitter do not allow children below the age of 13. However, this could be attributed to the rise in online learning where most children are now allowed to have smartphones hence they have access to those platforms.

Gender

Exposure to online threats is also linked to gender. Gender describes ideas and practices that constitute femininity and masculinity and these practices are socially constructed (Holmes, 2009). Men and women in this digital era are more active online and on each platform that can provide them with news, updates, current situations and stories. In terms of gender disaggregation, most of the respondents were female (65%) followed by males (35%). This is illustrated in figure 2 below.

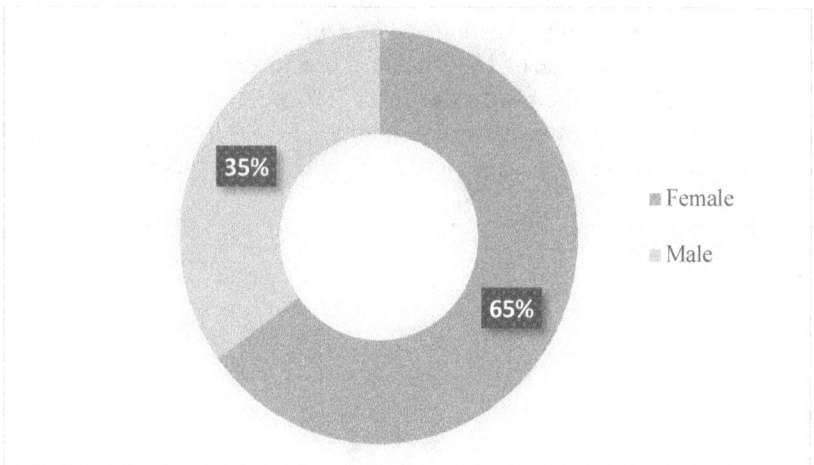

Figure 2. Gender of respondents

These statistics lead to the conclusion that since there are more women than men who are active online, by the same token, more women than men are experiencing online violence. The high number of female respondents may be linked to their keen interest in online safety as they are more vulnerable to trafficking, sexual harassment and abuse. Furthermore, females may have been spending more time online hence they were able to respond to the survey than their male counterparts.

Online violence includes sexual abuse, emotional abuse, and cyberbullying. These are the kinds of online abuse. As noted by Mishra (2021), cyber violence against women continues to be on the rise all over the world, sparing not even celebrities, social activists or news correspondents. In the same light, Budoo-Scholtz and Johnson (2023) affirm that the potential internet threats for African women accessing and using internet services are undeniable. Even though there are policies which protect women and girls from online violence, the predominantly African culture defames the character of those women who have been exposed to online attacks, especially when such attacks are inflicted by men.

Whilst Sustainable Development Goal Number 5 (SDG 5) emphasizes gender equality, deplorably, in Zimbabwe, the digital space records more women being sexually abused online. For example, there are countless unfortunate incidents whereby a woman's nude pictures have been leaked online and oftentimes, the patriarchal-oriented religio-cultural norms and values in Zimbabwe label this woman a prostitute. Paradoxically, if it is a man in a similar position, society does not judge him as harshly. In trying to keep up with current affairs, women spend more time online and they can have enough knowledge on how to protect themselves from online violence.

Hours spent on social media per day

The research results reveal that most of the respondents (75%), spend three hours or more per day on social media. This shows that social media is being embraced in Zimbabwe. As noted by Ponde-Mutsvedu and Chirongoma (2022), due to the advent of the Covid-19 pandemic, people started to frequently use social media for entertainment, online learning, socializing, evangelism, worship, online health services, and business activities. The interview results revealed that the use of communication technology has led to easy communication between people, whilst increasing the time people spend on social media platforms, which consequently contributes towards the increase of online abuse. Whether a person is using it for a good cause or not, security threats always happen on social media platforms. Hence, the more time children spend time on social media per day, the more they become vulnerable to cyber-attacks (Livingstone, 2020, Chirongoma and Ponde-Mutsvedu, 2021).

Social media platforms being used

The research results, illustrated in Figure 3 below, show that most people use WhatsApp platform (228), followed by Facebook (112). This is because WhatsApp is cheaper than any other social media platform, hence, most people prefer to use WhatsApp because data in Zimbabwe is expensive. Interview results also revealed that platforms like SnapChat and Tik Tok are less popular in Zimbabwe, therefore, a few individuals use these social media platforms.

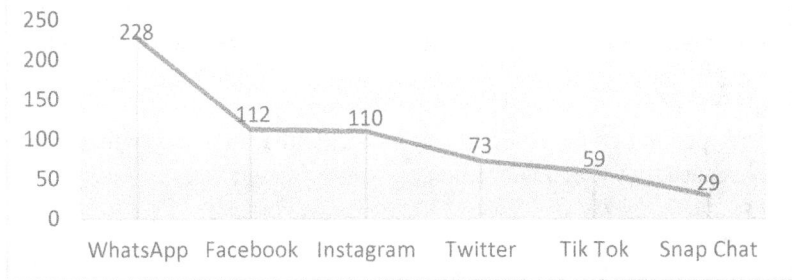

Figure 3. Social media platforms being used

Level of online safety

According to the research results as presented in Figure 4 below, 24% of the respondents feel safe online and can handle any threat or nuisance that comes their way. 39% are aware of the dangers associated with the use of social media, whilst 13% have encountered bad experiences which made them aware of the implications.

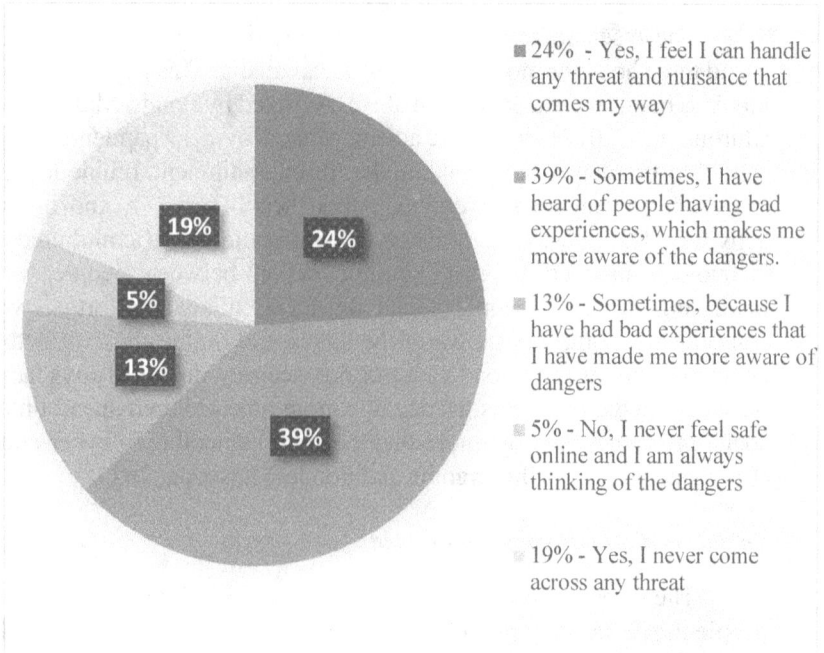

Figure 4. Level of online safety

The statistics presented above reveal that the more people become more aware of the dangers, the more they practice precautionary measures. Surprisingly, results from interviews show that some of the respondents feel that they have never come across any cyber threat. This might be indicative of the fact that they are ignorant of online threats; hence they do not really know whether they are under threat or not. Only 5% percent of the respondents indicated that they never feel safe online because they are always thinking of the dangers.

Biggest threat online

According to the research results presented in Figure 5 below, 121 of the respondents feel that the biggest threat online is that of strangers constantly approaching them online. 110 participants reported that they fear coming across sexual content whilst 108 mentioned that they are afraid of bullying and harassment. Some respondents reported that they fear being offered sexual content, someone using their phone to access inappropriate content and sites as well as peer pressure with a total amounting to 77, 83 and 42 respectively. Focus group discussions revealed that generally scammers constantly approach people online, especially on Facebook and can pose a security threat to people.

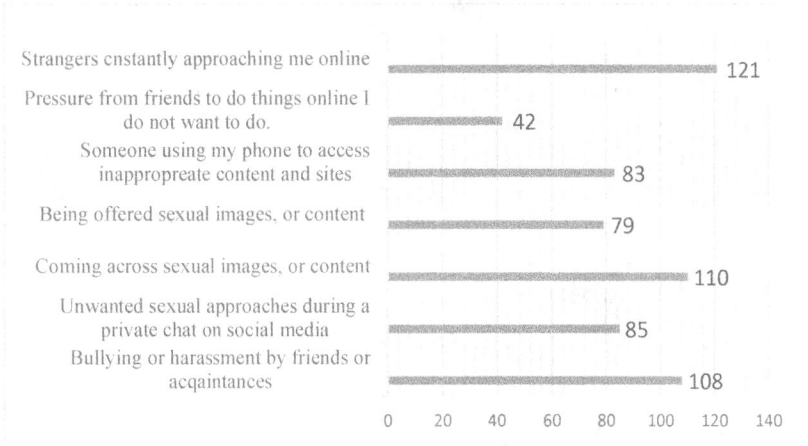

Figure 5. Biggest threat online

Number of times an individual added a stranger to online social networks

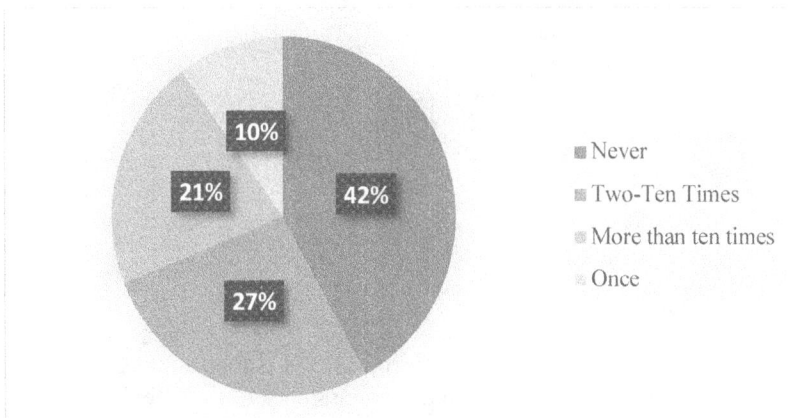

Figure 6. Number of times an individual added a stranger to online networks

Figure 6 above shows that 42% of the respondents have never accepted a stranger in their online networks. 27% said that they accepted a stranger on their social networks two to ten times whilst 21% did so more than ten times. Those who have once accepted strangers on their social networks were 10%. According to the interview results, most people are now aware of dangers online, hence, they try as much as they can to mitigate the associated risks.

Frequency of In-Person Meetings with Online Contacts

As illustrated in Figure 7 below, the majority (62%) of the respondents have never met in person with people they met on social networks. 20% said that they have met in person with the people they met on social media about two to ten times. 15% did that once, whilst 3% more than ten times. Focus group discussions revealed that people fear meeting up with strangers from their social networks because they are aware that strangers pose a security threat, hence, accepting to meet with strangers makes them vulnerable to cases like theft.

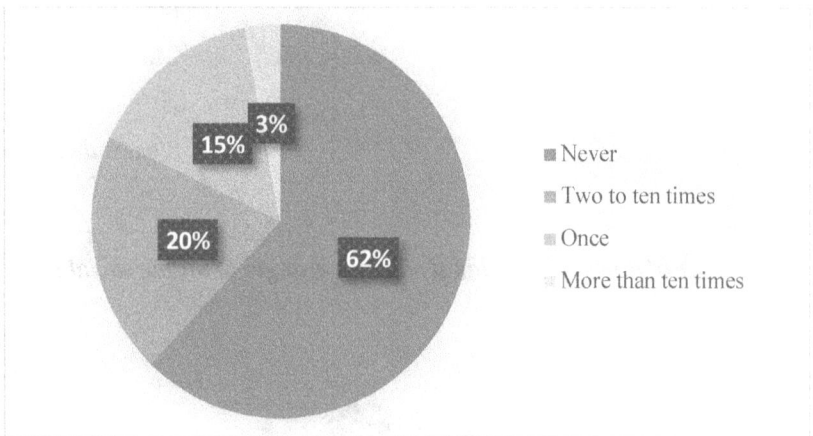

*Figure 7. Number of times a person met in person
with someone they first met online*

Reporting Cases

The results, as presented in Figure 8 below, show that 42% of the respondents reach out to their friends when they feel that they are vulnerable to online threats. 26% report to parents or guardians, and those who report to the police amounted to 17%. Only 12% mentioned that they have no one to report to. Interview results show that it may be easier to share challenges with friends than other people, hence, most respondents feel safe to share their stories with friends.

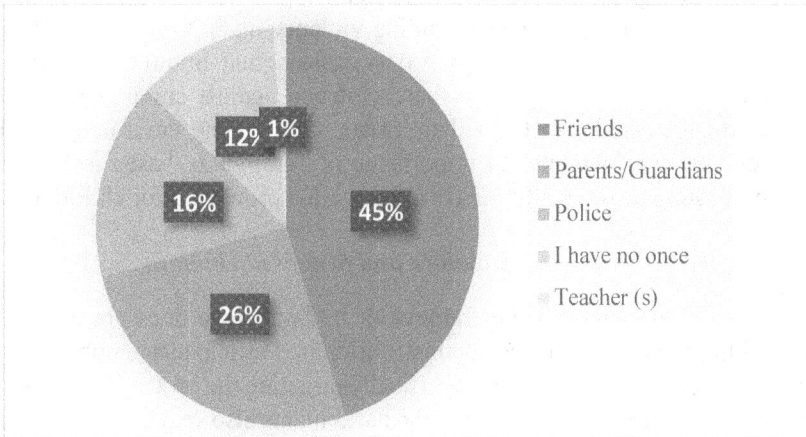

Figure 8. Where to report when you feel vulnerable online

Need for information on online safety

As illustrated in figure 9 below, 75% of the respondents indicated that they need more information on online safety. Only 25% mentioned that they did not need it. Results from interviews and focus group discussions indicated that awareness is still needed in the Zimbabwean communities on information on online safety. This will help the community to understand the dangers emanating from online or social networks as well as how to mitigate them.

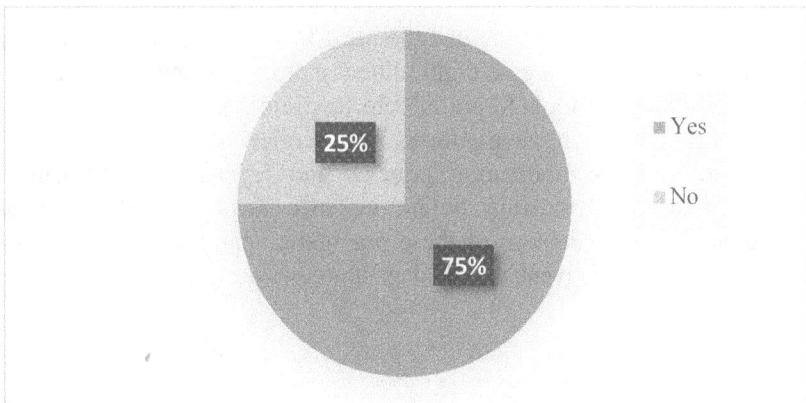

Figure 9. Need for information on online safety

Sociocultural Approaches to end child online violence

Many participants emphasized the importance of raising awareness about the harmful effects of online violence against children within the Zimbabwean society. They also suggested that traditional norms and cultural practices that perpetuate violence against children need to be challenged and transformed to create safer online environments. This reiterate the fundamental importance of community-based initiatives in promoting positive attitudes towards online protection for children.

Legal framework in Zimbabwe and proposed changes

The existing legal framework in Zimbabwe does not adequately address online violence against children. Participants emphasized the need for laws and policies specifically targeting the protection of children from online violence. Some of the participants also suggested the need for broadening the definition of child abuse to include online violence and to establish specialized courts to handle such cases.

Multi-stakeholder approach to end online violence against children

Participants stressed the importance of involving multiple stakeholders, including government agencies, civil society organizations, technology companies, educators, parents and children, in an endeavour to safeguard children against online violence. These propositions foreground the fundamental importance of collaboration and coordination among these stakeholders as a panacea for developing comprehensive strategies and effective interventions.

Pragmatic approach to end online violence against children

Participants highlighted the need for practical interventions, such as awareness campaigns, digital literacy programs and the development of technological tools to aid in detecting and reporting online violence. Engaging with online platforms and service providers to implement stricter content moderation policies and reporting mechanisms can contribute to mitigating online violence against children. Ongoing research and evaluation of these pragmatic approaches are essential to assess their effectiveness and adapt strategies accordingly.

Technology and Minors

Technology exposes minors and even adults to paedophiles, human traffickers, sexual abusers, drugs and even abductions. It is especially worrisome to note that children are spending more time on social media platforms for entertainment than for academic purposes. The research results revealed that children are spending more than 3 hours a day on social media, which makes them vulnerable to cyber-attacks. Children are familiar with most social media platforms, the majority spend time on WhatsApp, Facebook, Instagram and Twitter because they are cheaper as compared to TikTok. These results correspond with the findings made by Simani (2020) in a paper on Social Media Sites and Their Effect on Academic Performance, where it was revealed that 88% of students use WhatsApp because WhatsApp is attributed to being an instant message application that allows multitasking. Although social media platforms like WhatsApp and Facebook can be used for easy communication to conduct online learning and to promote remote learning, it is accompanied by negative effects such as the development of poor mental health as well as suicidal tendencies among children. Therefore, it is of primary importance for children to exercise their online rights to avoid cases of cyberbullying.

Some children (24%) feel safe on social media, and they feel that they can handle any threat that may come their way. Some of the respondents revealed that they have heard about the dangers, but they haven't experienced them yet, hence, they are taking precautionary measures. This position concurs with Mabvurira and Machimbidza (2022:99) who noted that online activities among children are associated with negative effects like children negatively influencing each other to cyberbully others which causes low self-esteem, poor mental health and suicidal tendencies among children. This shows that, although some children indicated that they feel safe online, this does not mean that parents or guardians should ever turn a blind eye to the threats associated with cyberbullying.

The children's biggest threat is being approached by strangers and scammers while others are afraid of sexual content. These results also complement Chiridza et al., (2016) who argue that although social media platforms like WhatsApp have brought an affordable communication platform, it is also susceptible to being abused by those who take advantage of its distinct features. This shows that social media can offer rampant communication of hoaxes and pornographic materials which are a threat to children. It is therefore clear that social media can expose children to certain cyber threats.

Even though some children do not accept strangers on their online networks, 58% are still willing to do so regardless of the implications involved. Moreover, 38% go the extra mile to meet strangers in person. This shows that these children are victims of safety risks and need to exercise caution and be mindful of the potential dangers such as meeting someone with malicious intentions or following victims to scam, fraud or kidnap.

The research results revealed that most children (45%) report to friends when they face an online threat. Some report to their parents (26%) and some do not report (12%) since they feel they have no one to report to. Children are reluctant to report to the police (16%), and their teachers (1%). This can probably be due to their preference of seeking peer support and support from friends whilst they fear some consequences like being labelled or falling into further bullying if they report to their teachers or authority figures like the police. Therefore, as argued by Mabvurira & Mandizvidza (2022:106), there is a need to educate children on online threats like cyberbullying and encourage them to report such cases without fear as well as conscientize the community at large on the threats associated with online activities so that they can minimize blaming the victims and discriminating them.

It was also discovered that 75% of children require information on online safety. This is important to protect them from online risks like online predators, inappropriate content and identity theft. Therefore, teaching children about online safety helps them to develop the knowledge and skills to protect them from the dangers of online violence, consequently making them responsible digital citizens.

Having detected such issues about safeguarding children against online violence, it becomes evident that teachers and parents are aware of what students are going through. This calls for the need for teachers to assist students through various initiatives to ensure that they are safeguarded against the devastating effects of online violence.

Recommendations

Based on the preceding discussion, the following recommendations should be noted:

- There is a need for further research on the types of vulnerabilities faced by children online.
- Children should be educated about online etiquette.

- The community at large needs to be conscientized about online violence so that they can minimise victim blaming and discrimination.
- The Government of Zimbabwe needs to enact more laws and policies on child online safety. So far, the authors of this chapter are aware of only two statutory instruments that prohibit the online abuse of children, these are, the Data Protection Act (Chapter 11:12) as well as the Censorship and Entertainment Control Act (Act 37 of 1967). However, there is still some ambiguity in terms of the sentencing that perpetrators can get if they commit these horrendous actions.
- There is need for the act to stipulate stiffer penalties for perpetrators of child online violence. Apart from paying hefty fines, the length of imprisonment for such people should be extremely high.
- The Government of Zimbabwe, through the Ministry of Justice, Parliamentary and Legal Affairs needs to gazette several bills that address child online protection for both the boy child and girl child, acknowledging the peculiar complexities that each gender faces when it comes to child online protection.
- There is a need for more than one reporting portal (hotline) to be established at a low cost so that it can be easily accessible to everyone, including those without access to the necessary mobile data.

Conclusion

The chapter examined the contemporary landscape of online violence against children in Zimbabwe. The issue of safeguarding children against online violence has become a pressing concern globally, including in Zimbabwe. Based on the results emerging from an online survey, this research has shed some light on various perspectives and approaches that are needed to address this problem effectively. The chapter noted that sociocultural approaches play a crucial role in ending child online violence. It has also established that addressing harmful gender norms and promoting positive values can help shape healthy and positive behaviours and attitudes towards children.

Legal framework in Zimbabwe needs to be strengthened to better protect children's online activities. Furthermore, there is a need for more explicit provisions on child online abuse as well as clear consequences for violators and legal avenues for victims to seek redress. Multi-stakeholder collaboration is necessary to tackle this issue. All key actors, including governments, civil society, the private sector and parents or caregivers should participate in interventions aimed at preventing and responding to online violence. Implementation of pragmatic strategies that understand the realities of cyberspace is vital. This approach should include promoting safe online practices for children, building digital literacy skills as well as supporting platforms that prioritize child safety. Moreso, embracing approaches which recognize the unique experiences of the different genders is key in safeguarding children against online violence. Cognizant of the disproportionate impact of online violence along gender lines, curbing gender-based violence is critical to protecting children, especially safeguarding girls from cyber-based violence.

This chapter has therefore presented evidence of the fact that curbing online violence against children requires a multipronged, comprehensive and collaborative approach which recognizes sociocultural aspects, legal frameworks, multi-stakeholder collaboration, pragmatic interventions and gender-considerate implementations. Through operationalizing such an approach, stakeholders can draw closer, developing a cyber-safe and more secure digital environment for children in Zimbabwe. Continued research and evaluation of pragmatic approaches become vital in assessing effectiveness and enhancing the creation of coping strategies accordingly.

References

AFRICAN CHILD POLICY FORUM, 2014. *The African Report on Violence Against Children.* Addis Ababa. http://srsg.violenceagainstchildren.org/sites/default/files/publications_final/african_report_on_vac/african_report_on_violence_against_children_2014.pdf.

BRONFENBRENNER Urie, 1979. *The Ecology of Human Development: Experiments by Nature and Design.* Harvard University Press.

CHIRONGOMA Sophia and PONDE-MUTSVEDU Lucia, 2021. "The Ambivalent Role of Technology on Human Relationships: An Afrocentric Exploration." In *African Values, Ethics and Technology: Questions, Issues and Approaches,* edited by Beatrice Dedaa Okyere-Manu, 155–172. Springer, Palgrave and Macmillan.

CHILD ONLINE SAFETY, 2019. *End Violence Against Children.* Human Dignity Foundation.

CRESWELL John and POTH Cheryl, 2016. *Qualitative Inquiry Research Design: Choosing Among Five Approaches.* Sage Publications.

EDBERG Mark et al., 2017. "Development of a Communication Strategy to Reduce Violence Against Children in South Africa: A Social-Ecological Approach." *The African Journal of Information and Communication.*

FEGERT Joerg and STÖTZEL Manuela, 2017. "Child Protection: A Universal Concern and a Permanent Challenge in the Field of Child and Adolescent Mental Health." *Child and Adolescent Psychiatry and Mental Health.*

GRAY Michelle, BLAKE Margaret and CAMPANELLI Pamela, 2014. "The Issue of Cognitive Interviewing Methods to Evaluate Mode Effects in Survey Questions." *Field Methods.*

HASANI Simani, "Social Media Sites Effect on Academic Performance: A Case of Zivezano High School." https://www.studocu.com/row/n/60052054?sid=01699730215

MABVURIRA Vincent and MACHIMBIDZA Dickson, "Cyberbullying among High School Learners in Zimbabwe: Motives and Effects." *African Journal of Social Work* 12, no. 3 (2022): 98–107.

MAGUIRE Moira and DELAHUNT Brid, 2017. "Doing a Thematic Analysis: A Practical Step-by-Step Guide for Learning and Teaching Scholars." *All Ireland Journal of Higher Education.*

PONDE-MUTSVEDU Lucia and CHIRONGOMA Sophia, 2022. "Tele-Evangelism, Tele-Health and Cyberbullying in the Wake of the Outbreak of COVID-19 in Africa." In *Religion and the COVID-19 Pandemic in Southern Africa,* edited by Fortune Sibanda, Tenson Muyambo, and Ezra Chitando, 103–114. London: Routledge.

SILVERMAN David, 2016. *Introducing Qualitative Research: Qualitative Research.*

VANESSA Gonye, "Internet Fueling Child Abuse: Police-NewsDay." *NewsDay,* December 4, 2022. https://www.newsday.co.zw/amp/local-news/article/200004990/internet-fueling-child-abuse-police.

Unsafe Abortion and Substance Misuse among adolescent street girls of the Harare Central Business District, Zimbabwe

Witness Chikoko

Introduction and background

Unsafe abortion and misuse of substances are some of the twin problems affecting children in street situations in many parts of the world. Substance abuse has been defined as taking drugs or substances for the wrong reasons (Makaruse, 2010). Substance abuse also includes taking too much of drugs or substances (Makaruse, 2010). In Durban, South Africa, street children face different forms of violence (Hills et al, 2016). Some face sexual abuse, violence and exploitation such as unprotected sex, raped among others (Hills et al, 2016). The metro police officers also meted physical violence in the form of harassment on the street children of Durban, South Africa (Hills et al, 2016).

Misuse of substances is also rampant among street children of Durban, South Africa (Hills et al, 2016). In Delhi, India, street children abuse substances such as alcohol, tobacco and inhalants (Dhawan et al 2020). The street children of Butwal municipality of Nepal misuse substances such as glue, cigarettes, gutkha (tobacco with betel nut), and alcohol among others (Sah et al, 2020). The following psychoactive substances are also common among street children in Mumbai, India (Gaidhane et al, 2008). These are nicotine, opioids, cannabis, alcohol and inhalants (Gaidhane et al, 2008). In a study of street children in Jimma town, Ethiopia, substance abuse is widespread (Ayenew et al, 2020). There is a multiplicity of factors that influence substance abuse among street children of Jimma Town, Ethiopia (Ayenew et al, 2020). Some of them include; fear of isolation, social networks, duration of homelessness, age, and gender among others (Ayenew et al, 2016).

In a study of homeless children and youth in the United States of America, there is a strong relationship between misuse of substances and sexual risk behaviours (Heerde and Hemphill, 2016). Some homeless children who were abusing substances were also vulnerable to sexual risk behaviours (Heerde and Hemphill, 2016). Some of the homeless children that were abusing alcohol, and amphetamine was also engaging in sexual behaviours such as anal sex, unprotected sex, and transactional sex among others (Heerde and Hemphill, 2016). Similarly, some of the street girls of the Harare Central Business District who were involved in commercial sex work also succumbed to misuse of substances (Chikoko, 2014 & 2017). The street girls used substance abuse to cope with the exploitative nature associated with commercial sex work (Chikoko, 2014).

On the other hand, misuse of substances also facilitated the adolescent street girls of Harare Central Business District to engage in multiple sexual relationships and commercial sex work among other sexual behaviours (Chikoko 2014 & 2017). Previous research findings by Ruparanganda (2008) noted that unsafe abortion was rampant among street children of Harare, Zimbabwe. He cited a case of a certain street girl, who had an unsuccessful abortion which almost killed her. In the case cited by Ruparanganda (2008), the dead foetus was decaying in the womb of the girl and this created several complications which resulted in her seeking modern medicine. The author added that some of the street girls had been using several medicines that included the *mukina*[1] tree, surf for washing and a bit of cement for unsafe abortion. However, Ruparanganda's (2008) study did not go deeper in terms of discussing how some of the street girls resorted to the use of psychoactive substances as a result of unsafe abortion.

However, previous studies on street children by Bourdillon from 1994 up to the present, Mhizha (2015), Mella (2012), Chikoko (2014; 2017 & 2023), Wakatama (2007), Ruparanganda (2008), Chirwa (2007), Chirwa and Wakatama (2000) have been limited in articulating the interrelatedness of the unsafe abortion and substance use among street girls of the Harare Central Business District, Zimbabwe in the face of adversities. In other words, there is a paucity of academic literature on the multi-dimensional nature of the misuse of substances and unsafe abortion of these children. The paper interrogates the multi-dimensional relationship between unsafe abortion and misuse of substances among adolescent street girls of the Harare Central Business District, Zimbabwe in the context of adversities.

---

[1] Mukina is one of the traditional medicines used for unsafe abortion

Feminist Social Work

The feminist approach explains the unequal power dynamics between men and women (Muridzo, 2014; Chikoko 2023). The approach explains that men and boys are socialised to dominate women and girls (Muridzo, 2014; Chikoko 2023). Thus, men and boys are expected to demonstrate their agency in public spaces. In addition, women are also socialised to be subservient and accept the dominance of their male counterparts (Muridzo, 2014). Women and girls are expected to be loyal and passive citizens and are sometimes confined in the private spaces of society. Therefore, patriarchy is responsible for the subjugation of women and girls (Chikoko, 2023).

Feminist social work is a specialised field of social work which promotes the empowerment of women and children among other vulnerable members of society (Wendt and Boylan, 2008). White (2006) observed that feminist social work is significantly influenced by other strands of feminism such as socialism, liberalism and Marxism among others. There are a number of characteristics that define feminist social work. Some of them include; redefining the private problems faced by women and girls as public issues (White, 2006). Feminist social work considers the societal issues affecting women and girls within the context of a wider socio-economic and political environment (White, 2006). The vulnerabilities of women and girls are a result of human interactions. Therefore, the solutions towards the empowerment of women and girls also lie within the broader societal human interactions, given the interdependent nature of human relations (White, 2006).

Feminist social work also acknowledges the agency and context of women and girls in society (Wendt and Boylan, 2008). In the case of adolescent street girls of Harare Central Business District, Zimbabwe, feminist social work takes note of the living circumstances of these girls. The living circumstances of the street girls that is characterised by multiple levels of vulnerabilities as a result of patriarchal structures and institutions. The patriarchal structures have marginalised and impoverished the adolescent street girls of the Harare Central Business District, Zimbabwe. The level of marginalisation and impoverishment is illustrated as adolescent street girls have limited access to sexual and reproductive health services.

Given such level and extent of marginalisation and impoverishment, the adolescent street girls of the Harare Central Business District, Zimbabwe demonstrate their agency in various ways such as misuse of substances and unsafe abortion among others. As adolescent street girls demonstrate their agency, they become vulnerable through the misuse of substances and unsafe abortion among others.

Ubuntu or Hunhu Philosophy

Abur and Mugumbate (2022: 22) argue that '*Ubuntu* has no specific place or date of origin but is expected to have originated in the West, Central and Northern parts of Africa and spread throughout the continent through migration that started 4000 years ago.' The *Ubuntu* or *hunhu* philosophy is a Pan-African perspective, that originated among the Bantu-speaking people (Smakange and Smakange, 1980). *Ubuntu* or *hunhu* philosophy has been passed on from one generation to another through oral forms (Abur and Mugumbate, 2022). Some of the oral forms included; song, poetry, dance, and storytelling among others (Abur and Mugumbate, 2022).

The *Ubuntu* or *hunhu* is also defined in a Zulu proverb, *umuntu ngamuntu ngabantu* (a person is a person through others) (Abur and Mugumbate, 2022; Mugumbate and Nyanguru, 2013; Shumbamhini, 2023). We are what we are through others (Mushunje, 2006). Abur and Mugumbate (2022: 22) observed that 'every individual is viewed through their family and the family is viewed through the extended family and tribe.' In *Ubuntu* or *hunhu* philosophy terms individualism is discouraged and thus not valued (Abur and Mugumbate, 2022). Kangethe (2023: 32) noted that, Ubuntu, 'advocates of humanity and in connectedness.'

The *ubuntu* or *hunhu* philosophy also defines the moral conduct among human beings (Mangena, 2007, 2012 & 2016). Some behaviours are defined by society as ethically good or acceptable (Mangena 2007). Some behaviours are not acceptable and are considered as '*kushaya hunhu*' (Chikoko, 2024). Such behaviours are condemned by society. Some of them include; sexual deviant behaviours like homosexuality, masturbation, multiple sexual relationships, commercial sex work, forced sex or rape among others (Chikoko, 2024). The unacceptable behaviours illustrate the lack of *Ubuntu* (Chikoko, 2024; Murove 2014). The *Ubuntu* has also been defined as the humanness of humanity (Van Breda, 2019). Humanness has implications that every person should treat others in a dignified manner (Murove, 2014; Mbigi, 2005; Mbiti 1995).

The *Ubuntu* or *hunhu* places values that are also considered useful by other cultures (Shumbamhini, 2023). Such values are regarded as virtues which demonstrate the humanness of humanity (van Breda, 2019). Some of the virtues include; fraternity, hospitality, worthiness, human

84

rights, social justice, tolerance, integrity, responsibility, fairness, reconciliation, reciprocity, gentleness, resilience, self-sacrifice, courtesy kindness, and bravery (Shumbamhini, 2023; Mupedziswa et al 2019; Tutu, 2012; Ramose, 2002; Shutte, 1993).

The *Ubuntu* or *hunhu* philosophy is also defined as a demonstration of group solidarity (Mushunje, 2006). Group solidarity is focal for the survival of African communities (Mupedziswa et al 2019; Mushunje, 2006). In line with *Ubuntu*, during times of poverty and deprivations, people were to survive through group care and not necessarily through individual self-reliance (Mupedziswa et al 2019; Mushunje, 2006). Therefore, when the adolescent street girls of Harare Central Business District, Zimbabwe engage in the misuse of substances and unsafe abortion, it demonstrates a lack of *Ubuntu* or *hunhu*.

The different Types of substances

Adolescent street girls of the Harare Central Business District, Zimbabwe misuse several substances. Some of them are psycho actives, traditional medicine, and aphrodisiacs among others. During in-depth interviews, one of the adolescent street girls of the Harare Central Business District, Zimbabwe indicated:

> We misuse several substances. Some of them are traditional medicine. For example, when I contract sexually transmitted diseases, we use such for treatment.

During informal conversations, one of the adolescent street girls also revealed that some of them were using *guchu* to clean their reproductive health systems. She said:

> Life is tough for us migunduru[2]. We use guchu to clean our reproductive health. Our reproductive health well-being is significantly influenced by the use of guchu.

During life history interviews, one of the adolescent street girls also indicated that they also misuse substances such as *chamba*[3] given the traumatic experiences they face daily on the streets of the Harare Central Business District, Zimbabwe. During field visits, the author interacted with several adolescent street girls misusing substances such as *guchu, chamba, chitongo*, among others. The author also saw some of the

---

[2] Migunduru refers to street children

[3] Chamba is cannabis

adolescent street girls engaging in sexual relationships in exchange for drugs with persons selling substances on the streets of Harare Central Business District, Zimbabwe.

One of the key informants, a street vendor also confirmed that adolescent street girls in the Harare Central Business District, Zimbabwe misuse a number of substances. He added that he has been selling a number of the substances to the adolescent street girls of the Harare Central Business District, Zimbabwe. He revealed that some of the substances misused included, traditional medicine, in aphrodisiac nature and psychoactive ones such as *chamba, chitongo* among others.

The use of traditional medicine to facilitate unsafe abortion

Some street girls in the Harare Central Business District use traditional medicine to facilitate unsafe abortion. One of the street girls died because of unsafe abortion. Pamela's friends revealed that she conducted unsafe abortions by mixing *mukina*[4] and other traditional medicines, which led to the rupture of her uterus. Although she was admitted at Harare Central Hospital, Pamela died of excessive bleeding.

The medical report also indicated that she was HIV positive. Her friends also added that Pamela was in the practice of conducting and orienting other girls on abortion on the streets. When Pamela died at the hospital, her body took two weeks before burial as there were some challenges. She did not have a birth certificate. To claim her body from the hospital was a big hassle for her family members. There were *lobola*-related issues as her family members were demanding payment from her street boyfriend. During the informal conversations, one respondent, Pamelas's friend, indicated that:

> Elder[5], the issue of unsafe abortion is something else. My friend Pamela passed died. She was a champion of unsafe abortion behaviours. She is the one who taught us all in the streets to do unsafe abortions but she was the one who became the victim. Pamela knew a lot of traditional medicines such as mukina[6]. Some of the medicines she got them from Epworth and Mbare[7]. Pamela aborted a pregnancy of twins and she subsequently died. She had bled profusely by the time

---

[4] Mukina is one of the traditional medicines used for unsafe abortion

[5] Elder refers to a researcher

[6] Mukina is one of the traditional medicines used for unsafe abortion

[7] Mbare is one of the oldest African townships established during colonial rule

Pamela was taken to Harare Central Hospital. That was something else. She just died when they arrived at the hospital. Pamela was living positively and she had killed many people. At Avondale, she contributed towards the death of the street boys in 2012. She also killed another one at Copa Cabana. Elder, nothing is happening at some of the hospitals. The nurses and doctors are more interested in money. These people are wicked. They cannot assist clients. After her death, there were many problems. Her boyfriend Freddy, whom she was cohabitating with on the streets, was supposed to pay lobola[8]. On the other hand, Freddy is someone who survives on selling marijuana and stealing only. Where could he find the money? Plus, Pamela did not have a birth certificate, so to take her corpse out of the hospital was very difficult. Social welfare and Streets Ahead officials had to intervene so that she could be buried.

During the informal conversations one of the street boys also revealed that, the street girls were using traditional medicines to do unsafe abortion. He said:

These girls that stay on the streets are witches, elder, they are real murderers. They are cruel, they kill their own children. They do not know that such children that they abort could be leaders like former President Mugabe. These children could take care of them in their future lives but ironically, they kill them. They get traditional medicines from elderly people of the Chawa tribe from Mbare, Epworth, and Mabvuku to use. So, if they continue doing that, they will face trouble. Pamela died because of that. As for me, whoever try to abort my baby will face it. Some of us we were treated when we were young. My grandmother is from Malawi and is of Chawa religion.

During the key informant interviews, a social worker employed by one of the Drop-in Centres revealed that unsafe abortion was rampant among street girls of the Harare Central Business District. She added that the street girls were using traditional medicine to facilitate unsafe abortions. The social worker also indicated that some of the street girls succumbed to death as a result of unsafe abortion.

Use of Detergent and Cement Concoctions for Unsafe Abortion

Some of the pregnant street girls used concoctions made up of washing detergents and cement to facilitate unsafe abortion. During the

---

[8] Lobola is bride price

informal conversations, one of the street girls revealed that she uses washing detergents and cement for unsafe abortion. She had this to say:

> Elder, when I got pregnant, I aborted using washing detergents and cement. I made the concoction then I drunk it. After a few hours, I had severe bleeding that led to the abortion. However, I regretted it afterwards as I lost a lot of blood. I even became unconscious as a result of the pain and bleeding process. One of my colleagues (*pointing to her friend*) took me to the hospital. Had it not been for her benevolence, I could have died from excessive bleeding elder (*sobbing*).

During the key informant interviews, one of the social workers indicated that some of the street girls were using a concoction made up of washing detergents and cement to facilitate unsafe abortion. The social worker added that as a result of unsafe abortion through the use of washing detergents and cement, some of the lives of the street girls were in danger.

Substance Use to Cope with Traumatic Experiences from Unsafe Abortion

Some of the street girls of the Harare Central Business District used substances to manage the traumatic experiences associated with unsafe abortion. During the informal conversations, she narrated that she became dependent on substance abuse after she had an unsafe abortion. She said the process of unsafe abortion traumatised her to the extent that she cannot forget it and to cope she has to abuse intoxicating substances such as *bhurongo*[9], *chapomba*[10] and *maragada*[11], among others.

She had this to say:

> I started taking substances after the traumatic experience I had during an unsafe abortion. I could have died. The pain that I went through was huge, so I prefer to stay drunk so as to forget that ordeal.

During the key informant interviews, a social worker employed by Streets Ahead revealed that some of the street girls became addicted to psycho active substances after unsafe abortion. She added that, the psychoactive substances assisted some of these girls in coping with their

---

[9] Bhurongo is cough syrup

[10] Chapomba is psycho active substance

[11] Maragada are tablets for mental health patients

traumatic experiences such as commercial sex work, unsafe abortion, and multiple sexual relationships among others.

Additionally, during the fieldwork visits, the author noticed that some of the street girls who were known for practising unsafe abortion were also addicted to psycho substances. Some of the psychoactive substances included *mbanje*[12], *bhurongo*[13] among others. In the street girls' bases, there were used bottles of *bhurongo*[14], cough syrup, and used condoms among others.

Unsafe Abortion and Substance Misuse

The social ills such as misuse of substances, and unsafe abortion among the adolescent street girls of the Harare Central Business District, Zimbabwe, illustrate their vulnerabilities as a result of patriarchal institutions or structures. The adolescent street girls of the Harare Central Business District are disempowered to the extent of misusing substances and practising unsafe abortion as a result of patriarchal socialisation. Patriarchal structures and institutions have significantly contributed towards, the abuse, violence and exploitation of the adolescent street girls of the Harare Central Business District, Zimbabwe.

The unsafe abortion among the adolescent street girls of the Harare Central Business District, Zimbabwe is a serious violation of human rights particularly access to sexual and reproductive health services. In terms of the provisions of CEDAW, article 12, women should have access to health services including family planning among others without stigma and discrimination (Munge, 2009). The United Nations Sustainable Development Goals also promote the empowerment of girls and women. In particular, SDG 5 fosters that all women and girls are protected from abuse, violence and exploitation thus gender equality (Chitando et al. 2023).

However, it becomes very debatable to provide family planning services to adolescent girls in the context of Zimbabwean culture. This is on the basis that children as minors in Zimbabwean culture are not expected to engage in premarital sex. As much as the Zimbabwean culture does not approve of premarital sex, the same is still very common among adolescent children in the country.

---

[12] Mbanje is cannabis

[13] Bhurongo is cough syrup

[14] Bhurongo is cough syrup

The adolescent street girls of the Harare Central Business District, Zimbabwe are vulnerable to abuse, violence and exploitation as a result of the patriarchal structures of the Zimbabwean society. Adolescent street girls are marginalised to the extent that they engage in unsafe abortion and misuse substances. The marginalisation of adolescent girls illustrates the level and extent of poverty, stigma and discrimination that unabatedly confront these children daily. The adolescent street girls of Harare Central Business District Zimbabwe are otherised and pushed to the periphery of mainstream Zimbabwean society. The marginalisation of adolescent street girls in the Harare Central Business District, Zimbabwe enunciate the extent of abuse, violence and exploitation within the broader socio-economic inequalities. Similarly, the adolescent street children of Durban, South Africa live in a context of vulnerabilities that are embedded in the national socio-economic inequalities (Osthus and Sewpaul, 2014). The gendered relations of the street children of Durban, South Africa are significantly influenced by structural influences particularly poverty (Osthus and Sewpaul, 2014). As a result of poverty, the street girls of Durban, South Africa look up to their male counterparts for provisions of basic needs such as food, and shelter among others (Osthus and Sewpaul, 2014). The subjugation of the adolescent street girls of Durban, South Africa is shown as they have limited access to basic services to the extent of engaging in commercial sex work or transactional sex to sustain themselves (Osthus and Sewpaul, 2014). The street boys also otherised their female counterparts by calling them derogatory names such as 'whore' (Osthus and Sewpaul, 2014).

Utilising the *Ubuntu* or *Hunhu* philosophy, substance abuse and unsafe abortion among adolescent street girls of the Harare Central Business District demonstrate social injustice among these children. The *Ubuntu* philosophy is about the humanness of humanity (van Breda, 2019). The humanness of adolescent street girls is severely affected when they engage in unsafe abortion and abuse of substances among others. Unsafe abortion and misuse of substances among adolescent street girls of the Harare Central Business District illustrate the lack of *Ubuntu* or *Hunhu*. However, who is to be blamed for the lack of Ubuntu among these adolescent street girls? (Chikoko and Ruparanganda, 2020) It is the society that is blamed for producing citizens or children who lack *Ubuntu* or *hunhu* (Chikoko and Ruparanganda, 2020). The otherised or subjugation of adolescent street girls negates the virtues of *Ubuntu* or *hunhu* philosophy. Such virtues as respect, social justice, and human rights are against the subjugation of the adolescent street girls of the Harare Central Business District, Zimbabwe.

The chapter has so far established that some of the street girls of the Harare Central Business District used traditional medicine to facilitate unsafe abortion. As highlighted above, the girls used traditional medicines such as *mukina*[15] for unsafe abortion. This shows that there several risks associated with unsafe abortion through misuse of traditional medicine. Similarly, in Cameroon, more than 40 % of emergencies admitted in some of the obstetrics and gynaecological hospitals were related to unsafe abortion (Munge, 2009).

Some of the adolescent street girls of the Harare Central Business District resort to the abuse of substances to cope with the traumatic experiences associated with unsafe abortion. The use of substances to cope with traumatic experiences by street girls also demonstrates that there are fewer or fewer services for children on the streets of the Harare Central Business District. This corroborates, the observations made by Hills et al (2016), where street children in Durban, South Africa resorted to the misuse of substances to cope with traumatic life experiences. The street children of Durban, South Africa resorted to abusing substances such as marijuana, alcohol, and smoking glue to manage difficult life experiences which were characterised by forced sex, physical violence, and scarcity of basic needs such as food among others (Hills et al, 2016).

Recommendations

The book chapter provides several recommendations to address unsafe abortion and substance abuse among the adolescent street girls of the Harare Central Business District. Some of the recommendations include the following;

- There is a need for full implementation of child rights laws, policies and programmes to arrest or curb or reduce substance abuse and unsafe abortion among street girls of the Harare Central Business District.

- To address childhood poverty, there is a need to strengthen the provision of social protection programmes among street children of the Harare Central Business District, Zimbabwe. For example, the implementation of a harmonised cash transfer programme to alleviate childhood poverty.

---

[15] Mukina is one of the traditional medicines used for unsafe abortion

- There is a need to promote accessibility and affordability of reproductive health services among street children of the Harare Central Business District,

- There is a need for free provision of condoms for street children. This could be debatable given the socio-cultural perspectives dominant in the Zimbabwean society,

- There is a need for the establishment of child-friendly reproductive health services targeting street children,

- There is a need for increased awareness raising for reproductive health services targeting street girls through platforms that are accessible to these children and

- There is a need to establish functional substance abuse rehabilitation centres on the streets of the Harare Central Business District, Zimbabwe. The functional substance misuse of abuse rehabilitation centres should be accessible to adolescent street girls among other vulnerable members of Zimbabwean society.

Conclusion

As discussed above, the book chapter concludes by arguing that there is a multi-dimensional nature of unsafe abortion and misuse of substances among the adolescent street girls of the Harare Central Business District, Zimbabwe in the face of adversities. Some of the adolescent street girls succumbed to unsafe abortion as a result of misuse of substances. Conversely, some of the adolescent street girls of the Harare Central Business District resorted to misusing substances as a result of the traumatic experiences associated the unsafe abortion. The unsafe abortion and substance-abusing behaviours among these children illustrate the marginalisation and impoverishment of these girls as a result of patriarchal structures and institutions. Given their living circumstances characterised by multilayered vulnerabilities, poverty, and unequal power dynamics, the adolescent street girls of the Harare Central Business District demonstrate their agency through the misuse of substances and unsafe abortion among others. On the other hand, utilising the Ubuntu or *Hunhu* philosophy, misuse of substances and unsafe abortion among the adolescent street girls of the Harare Central Business District illustrate the lack of *Ubuntu* or *hunhu*.

References

ABUR W. and MUGUMBATE J. R., 2022. "Experiences of Ubuntu and Implications of African Philosophy for Social Work in Australia." *Advances in Social Work Welfare and Education: Social Work in a Climate of Change* 23, no. 2.

ARMSTRONG L., 2014. "Screening Clients in a Decriminalised Street-Based Sex Industry: Insights into the Experiences of New Zealand Sex Workers." *Australian and New Zealand Journal of Criminology* 47, no. 2: 207–222.

ASANTE K. O., MEYER-WEITZ A. and PETERSEN I., 2015. "Mental Health and Health Risk Behaviours of Homeless Adolescents and Youth: A Mixed Methods Study." *Child and Youth Care Forum.*

AYENEW M., KABETA T. and WOLDEMICHAEL K., 2020. "Prevalence and Factors Associated with Substance Use among Street Children in Jimma Town, Oromiya National Regional State, Ethiopia: A Community-Based Cross-Sectional Study." *Substance Abuse Treatment, Prevention, and Policy* 15: 61.

BABBIE E. and MOUTON J., 2012. *The Practice of Social Research.* Southern Africa, Cape Town: Oxford University Press.

BOURDILLON M. F. C., 2009. *Children's Work in Southern Africa. Werkwinkel* 4, no. 1.

___, 1999. *Poor, Harassed but Very Much Alive: An Account of Street People and Their Organization.* Gweru: Mambo Press.

___, 1994. "Street Children in Harare, Africa." *Journal of the International African Institute* 4, no. 4: 516–533.

CHIKOKO W., 2014. "Commercial 'Sex Work' and Substance Abuse among Adolescent Street Children of Harare Central Business District." *Journal of Social Development in Africa* 29, no. 2.

___, 2023. "Exiting Commercial Sex Work: A Case of Adolescent Street Girls of the Harare Central Business District in Zimbabwe." *Journal of Human Rights and Social Work.*

___, 2024. "Ubuntu Philosophy and Sexual Behaviours in Zimbabwe: Implications for Social Work." In *Ubuntu Philosophy and Decolonising Social Work Fields of Practice in Africa,* edited by Janestic Mwende Twikirize, Sharlotte Tusasiirwe, and Rugare Mugumbate. London: Routledge.

CHIKOKO W. and RUPARANGANDA W., 2020. "Ubuntu or Hunhu Perspective in Understanding Substance Abuse and Sexual Behaviours of Street Children of Harare Central Business District, Zimbabwe." *African Journal of Social Work* 10, no. 1.

CHIKOKO W., CHIKOKO E., Muzvidziwa V. N. and RUPARANGANDA W., 2016. "Nongovernmental Organisations' Response to Substance Abuse and Sexual Behaviours of Adolescent Street Children of the Harare Central Business District." *African Journal of Social Work* 6, no. 2.

CHIRWA Y., 2007. "Children, Youth and Economic Reforms: An Expedition of the State of Street Children in Zimbabwe." In *Zimbabwe's Development Experiences since 1980, Challenges and Prospects for the Future,* edited by F. Maphosa, K. Kujinga, and S. D. Chingarande, 76–93. Ethiopia: OSSREA.

CHIRWA Y. and WAKATAMA M., 2000. "Working Street Children in Harare." In *Earning a Life: Working Children in Zimbabwe,* edited by M. F. C. Bourdillon, 45–58. Harare: Weaver Press.

CRESWELL J. W., 2014. *Research Design: Qualitative, Quantitative, and Mixed Methods Approaches.* 4th ed. Thousand Oaks, CA: Sage.

DHAWAN A., MISHRA A. K., AMBEKAR A., CHATTERJEA B., AGRAWAL A. and BHARGAVA R., 2020. "Estimating the Size of Substance Using Street Children in Delhi Using Respondent Driven Sampling." *Asian Journal of Psychiatry* 48: 101890.

DUBE L., 1997. "AIDS-Risk Patterns and Knowledge of the Disease among Street Children in Harare, Zimbabwe." *Journal of Social Development in Africa* 12, no. 2: 61–73.

___, 1999. *Street Children: A Part of Organized Society.* Unpublished D.Phil Thesis, Department of Sociology, University of Zimbabwe, Harare.

EYRICH-GARG K. M., O'LEARY C. C. and COTTLER L., B. 2008. "Subjective versus Objective Definitions of Homelessness: Are There Differences in Risk Factors among Heavy-Drinking Women?" *Gender Issues* 25: 173–192.

FARMER M., MCALINDEN A. and MARUNA S., 2016. "Sex Offending and Situational Motivation: Findings from a Qualitative Analysis of Desistance from Sexual Offending." *International Journal of Offender Therapy and Comparative Criminology* 60, no. 15: 1756–1775.

FLOYD L. and BROWN Q., 2012. "Attitudes Toward and Sexual Partnerships with Drug Dealers among Young Adult African American Females in Socially Disorganized Communities." *Journal of Drug Issues* 43, no. 2: 154–163.

GAIDHANE A. M., ZAHIRUDDIN Q. S., WAGHMANE L., SHANBHAG S., ZODPEY S. and JOHARAPUPKAR S. R., Substance abuse among street children in Mumbai. *Vulnerable Children and Youth.* Volume 3(1): 42-51, 2008.

HEERDE J. A. and HEMPHILL S. A., Sexual risk behaviours, sexual offenses and sexual victimisation among homeless youth: A systematic review of associations with substance use. *Trauma Violence & Abuse.* Volume 17 (05): 468-488, 2016.

HILLS F., MEYER-WEITZ A. and OPPONG-ASANTE K., The lived experiences of street children on Durban, South Africa: Violence, substance use and resilience. *International Journal of Qualitative Studies on Health and Wellbeing.* Volume 11, Number 01, 2016.

KANGETHE M. S., Perceptions of stakeholders on drivers of stigma subjected to people living with HIV/AIDS in Alice town, Eastern Cape: Implications for human rights and social service profession. *African Journal of Social Work.* Volume 13, Number 01, 2023.

MAKARUSE T., *Substance abuse among school children: A case study of Pafiwa High School in Mutasa.* unpublished MSW dissertation, Harare, School of Social Work, University of Zimbabwe, 2010.

MARSHALL B. D. L., The contextual determinants of sexually transmissible infections among street involved youth in North America. *Culture, Health and Sexuality.* 10 (8): 787-799, 2008.

MANGENA F., *Natural law ethics, Hunhuism and the concept of redistributive justice among the Korekore-Nyombwe people of Northern Zimbabwe: An ethical investigation.* unpublished D.Phil Thesis, Faculty of Arts, Harare, University of Zimbabwe, 2007.

___, *On Ubuntu and Redistributive punishment in Korekore-Nyombwe culture: Emerging ethical perspectives*, Harare, Best Practices Books, 2012.

___, African ethics through *Ubuntu:* A postmodern exposition. *Africology: The journal of Pan African studies* Volume 09, Number 02, 2016.

MBIGI L., *Ubuntu: The spirit of African transformation management*, South Africa, Knowres, Randburg, South Africa, 2005.

MBITI J. S., *Introduction to African Religion.* Heinemann, New Hampshire, 1975.

MHIZHA S., *The self-image of adolescent street children in Harare.* unpublished M. Phil Thesis, Harare, Department of Psychology, University of Zimbabwe, 2010.

___, Religious self-beliefs and coping vending adolescent in Harare. *Journal of Religion and Health* 53: 1487-1487, 2014.

___, The religious-spiritual self-image and behaviours among adolescent street children in Harare, Zimbabwe. *Journal of Religion and Health.* 54: 187-201, 2015.

MHIZHA S. and MUROMO S., An exploratory study on the school related challenges faced by street children in Harare. *Zimbabwe Journal of Educational Research.* Vol 25, Number 03, 2013.

MUNGE S. P., Substantive equality and women's rights to sexual and reproductive health in Cameroon. *Journal of Social Development in Africa* Volume 24, Number 02, 2009.

MUGUMBATE R. J., *Ubuntu:* An overview in Janestic Mwende Twikirize, Sharlotte Tusasirwe and Rugare Mugumbate (eds) *Ubuntu philosophy and decolonizing social work fields of practice in Africa.* London and New York, Routledge, 2024.

MUGUMBATE R. J. and NYANGURU A., Exploring African philosophy: The value of *ubuntu* in social work. *African Journal of Social Work* 3(2): pp 82-100, 2013.

MUGUMBATE R. J. and CHERENI, A., The theory of *Ubuntu* has its pace in Social Work. *African Journal of Social Work.* Volume 10, Number 1, 2019.

MURENJE M., Ubuntu and Xenophobia in South Africa's international Migration. *African Journal of Social Work.* Vol 10 Number 01, 2020.

MURIDZO N. G., Child sexual abuse in Zimbabwe: An Agenda for Social Work *The Indian Journal of Social Work.* Volume 75, Number 0, 2014.

MUROVE M. F., *Ubuntu Diogenes.* Volume 59 (3-4): 36- 47, 2014.

MUSHUNJE M. T., Child Protection in Zimbabwe: yesterday, today and tomorrow. *Journal of Social Development in Africa.* 21(1), 12-34, 2006.

MUPEDZISWA R., RANKOPO M. and MWANSA L., Ubuntu as a pan African philosophical framework for social work in Africa. In J. M. Twikirize and H. Spitzer (eds) *Social Work practice in African indigenous and innovative approaches* Fountain, Uganda, 2019.

RAMOSE M. B., *African Philosophy through* Ubuntu, Harare, Mond Books Publishers, 2002.

NEUMAN W. L., *Social research methods: Qualitative and quantitative approaches,* 7th edition, Boston, Pearson, 2011.

NYAMATHI A., HUDSON A., GREENGOLD B. and LEAKE B., Characteristics of homeless youth who use cocaine and methamphetamine. *The American Journal on Addiction.* 21: 243-249. 2012.

RUREVO R. and BOURDILLON M. F. C., Girls: The Less Visible Street Children of Zimbabwe, *Children, Youth and Environment.* 13(1):1-20, 2003a.

___, *Girls on the street,* Harare, Weaver Press, 2003a.

RUPARANGANDA W., *The Sexual Behaviour Patterns of Street Youth of Harare, Zimbabwe, in the Era of the HIV and AIDS pandemic.* unpublished Doctor of Philosophy Degree Thesis, Harare, Sociology Department, University of Zimbabwe, 2008.

SAH S. K., NEUPANE N., PRADHAN A., SAH S. and SHARMA A., Prevalence of glue sniffing among street children. *Nursing Open* 7 (206-211), 2020.

SAMKANGE S. and SAMKANGE T. M., *Hunhuism or Ubuntusim*: A Zimbabwe Indigenous Political Philosophy, Harare, Graham Publishing, 1980.

SHUTTE A., *Philosophy for Africa.* South Africa, University of Cape Town, 1993.

TUTU D., *No future without forgiveness,* Random House, South Africa, 2012.

OSTHUS I. S. and SEWPAUL V., Gender, power and sexuality among youth on the streets of Durban: Socio-Economic realities *International Social Work.* 1 (12), 2014.

TADELE G., "Unrecognized victims"; Sexual Abuse against Male Street Children in Metkato Area of Addis Ababa. *Ethiopian Journal, Health Development,* 23 (3), 2009.

VAN BREDA A. D., Developing the notion of Ubuntu as African Theory for Social Work Practice. *Social Work/ Maatskaplikewerk*, Vol 55 No.4 Issue 6, 2019.

WAKATAMA M., 2007. *The Situation of Street Children in Zimbabwe: A Violation of the United Nations Convention on the Rights of the Child (1989).* Unpublished D.Phil thesis, School of Social Work, University of Leicester, United Kingdom.

WENDT S. and BOYLAN J., 2008. "Feminist Social Work Research Engaging with Poststructuralist Ideas." *International Social Work* 51, no. 5: 599–609.

WHITE V., 2006. *The State of Feminist Social Work.* London and New York: Routledge, Taylor and Francis Group.

The Dynamics Promoting the Escalation of Street Children in the Streets of Harare, Zimbabwe, and the Social Work Responses

Francis Maushe, Etiya Edith Chigondo, Mangwiro and Witness Chikoko

Introduction

Children living in the streets are a big reason to worry about considering the rights and welfare of children in Zimbabwe. Research evidence and media reports have highly pointed out key factors that fuel high rates of street children as extreme poverty, drug and substance abuse, and HIV/AIDS. Manungo (2018) argues that push factors such as socio-economic challenges encourage children to become street children. The burden of street children in the world has resulted in the creation of a unique substructure society that is characterized by specific norms and values (Kanjanda & Chiparange, 2015). Several researches have established that the influx of street children globally is commonly a result of different factors such as neglect, abuse, poverty, and harsh conditions due to the loss of parents. According to Kanjanda & Chiparange (2015), the world today contains about 150 million children who live in the streets which is a very huge number that demands action from the world. Compas Children's Charity (2023) states that the world contains a total of 2.2 billion which implies that 1.5% of the children live in the street. Given the large number of children who live in the streets, the conditions they are exposed to are fascinating some live in temporary open environments in which they spend their time begging, hawking, or selling to make some money to find food to eat (Compass Children's Charity, 2023).

A global picture of street children is based on various facets (Consortium for Street Children, 2018). The rate at which the number of street children is increasing in the streets is most worrying for child protection efforts. The chart below labelled (Figure 1) gives a global picture of street children based on various aspects.

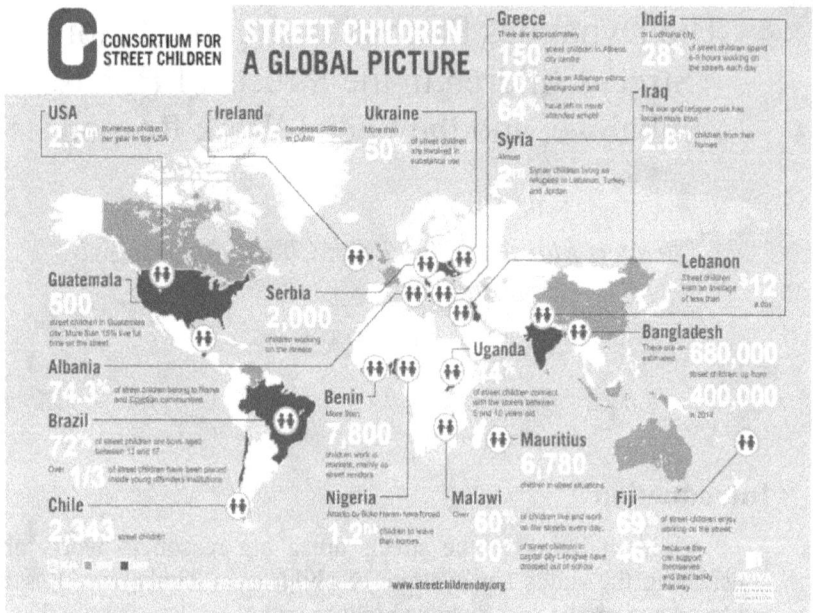

Figure 1. Global picture of street children.
Source: CFSC_Map 2016.indd (childhub.org)

As shown in Figure 1, Iraq contains about 2.8 million street children who fled their homes because of war and the refugee crisis. Secondly, the USA contains about 2.5 million homeless children who live on the streets. Nigeria has a total of 1.2 million children who live in the streets after the Boko Haram attacks. Bangladesh is the third highest with 680,000 children living in the streets. Nigeria appears to be one of the African countries with the highest number of street children.

The lives of street children in Iran were assessed based on survey findings from six major cities (Vameghi, Payam, Gholamreza, Marzieh & Giti, 2023). It was established that street children are most marginalized based on the severe conditions they are exposed to. In this regard, Vameghi et al. (2023) established that 90% of the street children were boys and the majority of them were aged between 10 and 14 years. Based on the major six cities that were surveyed, Vameghi et al. (2023) argue that most children (75.5%) survived by working about 5 hours a day vending to get themselves a living. The causes of children living on the street have been attributed to a combination of socio-economic factors, such as high levels of unemployment, family poverty, increasing levels of union instability and dissolutions, lack of family support systems, high virus (HIV) prevalence, substance abuse and domestic violence (Mokomane & Makaoae, 2015). Notably, the major challenges that street children experienced obtained from the survey included: harsh weather conditions, police repression, insults and beatings from people, and starvation.

The problem of street children in Indonesia is also more pronounced given the array of problems that these children experience in the streets. A survey of street children in Depok Master School established that street children work as child labourers to earn a living on the road (Bahar et al. 2019). The UK and USA also have a high number of street kids who fled their homes for various reasons. The major reasons that influence street children in the UK were found to be childhood adversities (Fekadu & Anula, 2020).

The lives of street children in Pakistan appear to be a double-edged sword in which some of the problems that fuel children to leave their homes are also haunting them on the streets. A good number of children in Pakistan fled their homes because of getting involved in sexual abuse and they joined the streets where sexual abuse is also very high (Bahar, Zainudin, & Hanny, 2019). It was established that about 80% of street children engage in sexual intercourse in the majority of girls are involved in commercial sex work. High levels of sexual exploitation in the streets are believed to be drivers of HIV/AIDS and Sexually Transmitted Infections (STIs) worsening the vulnerability of street children. Social workers' intervention in Nigeria has been called for given the country's largest rate of street children due to the Boko Haram attacks (Otigba, 2022). A qualitative study that focused on Lagos state established that live in unprecedented conditions such as exposure to violence, sexual, and physical abuse, behaviours with serious medical consequences, and drug and substance abuse (Ndulo, 2022). The implications of street children in Nigeria were explored in the major issues that were raised were that children who grow up in streets lack the vital parenting elements resulting in undesirable behaviors such as high involvement in crime. Streetism is a heavy blow to the economy of Nigeria posing a big social and economic problem even to other parts of the world.

The lives of children were a menace during the COVID-19 era in the streets of Uganda. According to Kawala, Kirui & Cumber (2020) street children in Uganda experienced the worst situations including police brutality and hunger since they were unable to do vending activities due to Covid-19 restrictions. Covid-19 disproportionately exacerbated the vulnerability of street children in Uganda. The conditions that street children are exposed to are burdensome.

The image above shows children begging for food in the streets of Uganda. This situation is not alien to Zimbabwe which also boasts a high number of street children based on various factors that influence this burden. The experiences of street children in Zimbabwe are disheartening based on the fact that the number is increasing to unprecedented levels (Ndhlovu & Tigere, 2022). Manungo (2018) argues that there are many children in the streets of Harare, 62% of these children slept in the streets while 38% slept both at home and in the streets. Zimbabwe experiences a large number of street children in its major towns with Harare, Gweru, Mutare, and Bulawayo hosting big numbers (Ndhlovu et al., 2022). Efforts have been made to establish long-lasting solutions to curb streetism but a lot of challenges are faced. The dangers that street children are exposed to are divorced from the dictates of various legislative frameworks that support child protection measures. Several media houses and activists among other stakeholders have been focusing on the challenges being faced by street children in Harare with the major problems being physical and sexual abuse on the part of girls, though boys are also likely to be abused, not going to school, lack of access to food, and harsh weather conditions as well as police brutality among other problems.

Despite the existence of the various challenges that street children face, efforts have been put in place in Zimbabwe. However, the rising number of street children are red flag regarding the efficacy of the interventions in place to curb the rise of street children in Harare. The government and several stakeholders have initiated different interventions to curb the problem of street children, including; social protection programmes and other food distribution schemes. Figure 2 below shows children in the streets of Harare facing the chilling winter times.

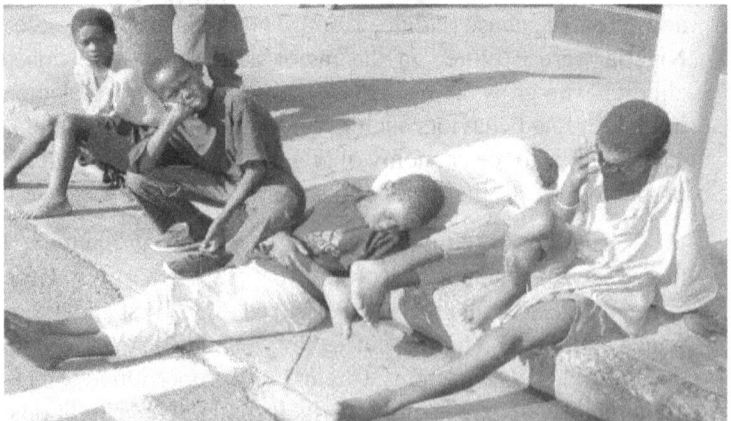

Figure 2. Children in the streets of Harare during chilling winter
Source: Harare's Street kids endure chilling winter - NewsHawks

Children in the streets encounter very tough conditions sleeping in the open with no blankets or warm clothes as well as having no guarantee that they will find something to eat the next day. The protection of street children in Zimbabwe has been heavily criticized by the existing programmes that are failing to curb the increase in children who join the streets as well as reduce the challenges that these children encounter in the streets. This boggles the mind to say why the streets remain a destination for children from homes in Harare. Existing literature still does not contain convincing data about the factors that are causing the increase in street children and why the existing measures are not reducing the number of street children. The arena of streetism is narrowly researched in Zimbabwe. The chapter is premised on these objectives; to assess the factors that contribute to the increase of street children in Harare and to explore the interventions that can be implemented to curb the increase in street children. Therefore, this chapter assess the factors contributing to the increase of street children towards coming up with sustainable solutions to curb street children and protect those who already live on the streets.

Social Constructivism Theory

The social constructivism theory explains the interaction between children and their environments. According to the major tenets of this theory, street children experience various situations (multiple realities) and these should be considered to figure out ways to help the children out through effective protective measures (Amineh & Dettlaff, 2020). Children can experience unwelcome situations in their homes such as abuse from parents, and step-parents among other caregivers, and leave their homes to live in the streets to free themselves from conflict between their lives and the environment they live in. Girls can experience sexual abuse at home and end up leaving their homes to live on the streets while they can also experience harsh conditions in the street environment.

Presentation of Biographical Data and Experience

The biographical information that was gathered from participants is presented in this section. The data includes gender, highest professional qualifications, age, and source of living for the participants. Tables and charts were used to present and interpret biographical data for the study. The work experience of the professional staff who were involved in this study was presented in the form of the Table 1 below.

Work experience for professionals	Frequency
0-5 years	17
6-10 years	44
10years and above	10

Table 1. Work Experience for the Professional Staff

Table 1 shows that four of the professional staff had experience between 0-5 years, 2 had between 6 and 10 years of experience, as well as the remaining 12 had above 10 years of experience. Thus, the majority of the professional staff had adequate years of experience working with street children.

Age, sex, years in the streets, and highest grade/form attended

The study solicited the biographical data of the street children in terms of their age, sex, years in the streets, and the highest grade or form they reached. The results were presented in the form of the Table 2.

Bio	Variables	Frequency
Age	8-10 years	3
	11-13 years	11
	14 years & above	4
Sex	Males	13
	Females	5
Years in the streets	0-6 months	2
	7-12 months	4
	1-2 years	5
	More than 2 years	7
Highest grade/form attended	Primary level	12
	Secondary level	5
	Never been to school	

Table 2. Age, Sex, Years in the streets, and highest grade attended by street children. Source: Interviewed Street Children

The table shows that 3 out of 18 were aged between 8 and 10 years, 11 out of 18 were aged between 11 and 13 years, and 4 out of 18 were above 14 years of age. The street children distribution in terms of age shows that the children were able to provide detailed explanations about the factors that drove them to join the streets as well as describe the challenges they face in the streets. The children's distribution in terms of sex was solicited, as shown in Table 1, 13 out of 18 were boys while the remaining 5 out of 18 were girls. The distribution shows that more boys are living in the streets as compared to girls.

The table shows that 2 out of 18 of the street children have been on the streets for a period between 0 to 6 months. 4 out of 18 have been in the streets of Harare for about 7 to 12 months, 5 out of 18 have been in the streets for a period between 1 and 2 years. The remaining 7 out of 18 highlighted that they have been on the streets for more than 2 years. The data shows that the majority of the interviewed street children have been in the street for a considerable time making it prudent for the chapter to have gathered truthful and authentic findings about street life and the factors that influenced them to join the streets.

It was obtained that 12 out of 18 of the street children reported that they reached primary school level as the highest level of education. Five (5) out of 18 of the street children reported that they have secondary education as their highest educational achievement while 1 out of 18 reported that he has never been in school. The majority of the street children at least attended schools and were able to comprehend the questions that they were asked in the interviews to provide insightful responses on the factors that influenced them to leave their homes and live in the streets.

Factors that contribute to street children

Most of the professional staff and street children outlined the major factors that influence children to leave their homes and join street life to include extreme poverty, child abuse and neglect in the home environment, family breakdown (divorced parents), dropping out of school, behavioural and mental disorders, death of parents, and peer pressure and there are discussed below.

Extreme poverty

Extreme poverty remains one of the factors that influence children in urban areas to live on the streets. The majority of the interviewed participants indicated that abject poverty in which children can fail to secure a meal the whole day or just have one meal pushes them to join the streets to beg to fill their stomachs. Some of the interviewed participants highlighted the following:

> From our experience with working with street children, extreme poverty (hunger) scares children to leave their homes anticipating getting food from begging in the streets (Interviewed Professional Staff).

> Children can be pressured to leave their homes and just go for example some girls have been found to have left their homes and join child prostitution in which they get money from money in compensation for transactional sex (Interviewed Professional Staff).

> Hunger is sometimes associated with stigmatization in which children even drop out of school and join the streets in fear of being stigmatized and think they might earn a living in the streets (Interviewed Professional Staff).

From the above responses, it was shown that extreme poverty is a key driver for children to join the streets of Harare anticipating to get a better living.

Child abuse and neglect in the home environment

Child abuse and neglect are some of the factors that contribute to street children in Harare. The street fled abusive home environments. The most prominent forms of abuse that were highlighted were physical abuse, child labour, and sexual abuse of girls. One of the interviewed professional staff highlighted that:

> Girls who were staying with extended families and step-parents experienced sexual assaults and were threatened not to report the matters and they resorted to living in the streets in Harare. For example, one girl said that her stepfather forced himself on her while she was in grade 6. Unfortunately, when she joined the streets, she was introduced to prostitution in which they host a group of men for transactional sex.

A key informant noted that:

> Some boys whose parents passed on were subjected to harsh conditions by relatives in which they were heavily beaten, deprived of going to school, and scolded, for example, being labelled an orphan. One would be told, "Go and tell your concerns to your parents at their graves" of which the extended family members would be enjoying the properties left while depriving the surviving children.

> I was made to work as a farm worker in tobacco fields and my uncle would collect the money and use it to drink beer. I had no clothes and would be deprived of food at home despite having been at work (Transcribed Child's Voice)

Children are forced to join street life because of the very harsh conditions they are exposed to in their home environments. Experiencing challenges such as child labour, heavy beatings, emotional abuse, stigmatization, and restrictions to basic needs such as food and clothes influence most children to leave their homes and join the streets.

Family breakdown (divorced parents & death of parents)

Broken homes highly contribute to street children. Some of the street children emanate from broken homes in which their parents divorced or have died and children are left in unpleasant situations with stepmothers/fathers or extended family members or siblings. This can be regarded to be a huge push towards the exodus of children from their homes to the streets.

Dropping out of school

Dropping out of school is also a push factor for children to join street life. The majority of the professionals who have directly worked with street children explained that children drop out of school because of a lack of support from the home in which they walk long distances and spend the day with empty stomachs. During the interviews, one professional indicated that:

> One of the boys who I know in the streets of Harare indicated that he dropped out of school because he was supposed to come back from school and go to the fields or look after cattle without eating anything. Also, he indicated that he never wore a school uniform at his former rural school and his peers would laugh at him. By feeling disgraced and discriminated he dropped out of school and traveled to Harare on foot from Mhondoro".

Thus, dropping out of school due to a harsh living environment for children influences them to think living in the streets is the best option. Unfortunately, it is not certain that children will find comfortable environments on the streets since the streets also contain challenges for the children.

Behavioural and mental disorders

Behavioural and mental disorders were also found to be a major cause for children to increase in the streets of Harare. Children who are involved in antisocial behaviours are more likely to leave their homes and stay on the streets. it was also revealed that some children especially boys engage in drugs and substance abuse at a tender age resulting in them leaving their homes to exercise independence to do what they want while living on the streets. Additionally, mental disorders are regarded by the professional staff to be another fact that influences the children to leave the streets. Some children have traits of mental illness such that they cannot interact well with peers, family, or even at schools and consequently they go to stay in the streets and survive by eating in bins and begging or stealing from passersby in the streets.

The main source of living

In some cases, street children survive by vending (selling biscuits, sweets, cigarettes, and other items), begging, and shoplifting. One of the interviewed street children had to say that:

> Most of the time we survive by begging for food and money from people in the streets of Harare *but sometimes we get meals from Street Ahead offices, especially on weekends. Ndinowana mari yekutenga chikafu after ndatengesa maswteets nemabiscuits angu pamarobots.*
>
> Sometimes I also get gifts from *vanodarika nemota dzavo* [I buy food after getting profits from selling sweets and biscuits in the streets mainly road intersections/robots. [Sometimes I receive gifts like food and money from motorists. (Interviewed Street Child).

Children get their living from mainly vending and begging. It was highlighted that they also get some meals, particularly during weekends from Street Ahead.

Services provided by the stakeholders to street children

In some contexts, professional staff provide the key services to street children in Harare including services; meals for the street, children counselling services and donations of clothes. Streets Ahead (an organization which deals with children in the streets) said, 'that they also provide adoption, fostering and family reunification'. The services the organizations provide to street children are meant to reduce the problems that these children face. However, it was found that stakeholders are failing to meet the demands of street children in a way that protects them, promotes their well-being, and establishes places of safety for these children.

Challenges encountered in the streets by the children

There are several challenges that are encountered by street children in Harare. The major challenges include physical abuse, sexual abuse, hunger, and exposure to diseases.

Physical abuse

Children in the street experience physical abuse. The responses below were captured during the interviews:

> Street children are beaten by older street boys who would want to forcefully take their food (Interviewed Professional)

> Children are physically assaulted by other street children fighting for places to sleep at night in the streets (Interviewed Professional).

> Police brutality is one of the challenges faced on the streets. Also, security guards are reported to be physically abuse us beating us if we try to find a place to sleep near the buildings they guard (Transcribed Child's Voice).

This shows that the streets are not a haven for children yet they left their homes because of abuse among others and they also face the same fate in the streets. Physical abuse for children remains high in the streets of Harare.

Sexual abuse

Sexual abuse remains a prominent challenge that is faced in the streets of Harare. Young girls are the most affected population. They are sexually abused by other street children, security guards, and other older men who molest and solicit sexual favours from the young street girls. On the other hand, cases of sodomy in the streets exist in which the boys are being sodomized even by older men and their peers.

Hunger

Children in the streets survive by begging, vending, and stealing. The children experience extreme hunger because they are not guaranteed meals in the streets. They could spend the whole day without getting a single meal. Thus, children end up eating food from bins which is not safe for human consumption.

From the 18 street children who were interviewed, 15 out of 18 indicated challenges such as brutality and assaults from police and security guards, sexual abuse, and exposure to diseases due to harsh weather conditions. One of the street children said:

> Most times the police beat us with mboma. Maguard anotidzinga kuti tisarara mumadziro emashop. Nguva yakawanda tinodzingirirwa tichinzi muri mbavha…life yemustreet marwadzo kuti titodya kutokumbira mota dziri kudarika pamarobots. [Most times the police beat us to leave the streets as well as the security guards who beat us if we find a place to sleep in shop verandas. We get accused of being thieves even if we reach out to seek help. We survive from begging from motorists at road intersections (Robots)].

Another child narrated shedding tears;

> *I was raped by one of the security guards and he offered me bread to eat. I am in pain, I left our home after being chased away by my uncle after the death of our parents. I also dropped out of school and the only option was to come to Harare. I now sleep with different men especially security guards and other men in exchange for food.*

Showing much depression another child revealed that:

> *Tinotonhorwa nekunaiwa nguva yemvura especially muCovid vamwe vedu vakarwara vakafa. Zvinotirwadza kuti tinosvika rinhi tichigara mustreet chando chichiperera pamuviri tisina magumbezi chero zvekupfeka hatizviwane. I sometimes sell masweets asi vanhu vanondisema hanzi hatitengi pamunhu ane tsvina. [We are exposed to very harsh conditions sleeping in the cold. During the Covid-19 era, some of our peers died of Covid-19. We do not have places to sleep or blankets and even we are always dirty. I sell sweets but very few people would want to buy from a person with much dirt].*

Clearly, street children are exposed to very tough conditions that affect their well-being and developmental milestones. The challenges that children experience in the streets expose the extent to which children are abused and neglected both in their homes and in the streets. No indication of child protection was highlighted during the interviews with the children. On the contrary, the police who should be custodians of children were cited to be the ones exacerbating the abuse of children by beating them and chasing them away exposing the children to more dangers of the streets.

Interventions and Social Work's Response to Prevent Streetism

In light of the factors that contribute to street children and the challenges the children experience in the streets; major interventions can be implemented to improve the well-being of children and safeguard children's rights. The interventions were mainly centred on social work's response to streetism in the streets of Harare. Most of the children who were interviewed indicated that they are not safe and they are struggling to make a life as compared to other children who live in comfortable home environments. Overlay, street children need protection and support to address hunger, protect them from abuse, access to decent shelter, access to adequate meals, and access to education. The suggestions from the street children for the above areas to be addressed for their lives to take an ordinary shape. Social work's response to these challenges faced in the streets and the situations that influence children to leave their homes to join the streets can flatten the curve and change children's narrative in the streets of Harare.

Moreover, the significance of social work in addressing the plight of street children in Harare requires particular attention. An important intervention is to eradicate streetism in Harare by addressing both push and pull factors. Resources should be mobilized such that all the street children should be placed in safe havens such as childcare institutions and emergency shelters. The need to protect children from the hell of the streets was emphasized by the professional staff during the interviews.

The Department of Social Service should embark on a nationwide assessment of children in homes to figure out those children who are facing unpleasant circumstances such as abuse and are on the verge of joining the streets. Moreover, institutions such as schools and churches can be used to identify abused children in their homes. The use of child protection committees, health workers, and local leaders is highly effective in the identification of child abuse and other factors that cause children to join street life. In the same vein, the strengthening of law enforcement was cited to be used in conjunction with home assessments to maximize the protection of children in their homes to prevent streetism.

Dynamics Promoting the Escalation of Street Children in the Streets of Harare

In terms of push factors, children are driven into streets by extreme poverty at home, parental abuse/violence, lack of family support, family breakdown, abuse by step-parents and death of parents or guardians (Nathan & Fratkin, 2018; UNODCCP, 2001; Diriba, 2015).

Factors contributing to the increase of street children

The major factors that were highlighted include: extreme poverty, child abuse and neglect in the home environment, family breakdown (divorced parents), dropping out of school, behavioural and mental disorders, death of parents, and peer pressure. Children leave their homes to join the streets because of extreme poverty in which they lack access to decent meals and do not have access to their school needs. This is in synch with Shitindi (2023) who studied the influence of poverty on streetism of children in Dar Es Salaam and Dadoma cities. Dutta (2018) notes that extreme poverty was the primary cause of the increasing number of street children in India. This shows that poverty has become the biggest challenge faced by children and their families which forces them to stay in the streets. According to Ward and Seager (2010), the issue can only be reduced through preventive initiatives by reducing the number of families living in poverty and supporting families so they can raise their children safely. Thus, coming up with preventative measures that support the parents, guidance and the children can reduce the number of children living and working in the streets.

Child abuse was another factor contributing to children living and working on the streets. This is in agreement with the literature by the Consortium for Street Children, (2018) which states that the extent to which children experience child abuse and neglect in the home environment and decide to join the streets is one of the factors that is being noticed in many developing countries. Several studies obtained similar findings that children flee their homes due to harsh home environments. Ethiopian streets are flooded with street children who fled their homes due to physical and sexual abuse by relatives (Endris & Sitota, 2019). Ward and Seger (2010) state that within the interviews with children concerning push factors, the girls described sexual abuse by stepfathers, while boys described irritated relationships with step-parents. Abusive environments scare children to leave and try new homes. Thus, there is a need for all stakeholders to assist in placing children in a place of safety if their homes are not conducive enough to protect them from harm.

However, Endris & Sitota (2019) argue that some children join the street because of undesired behaviours such as smoking drugs such as Crystal Meth, Cannabis, chewing chats, and sniffing among others as was found in Ethiopia. Additionally, Uduigwomen (2019) established similar findings that were produced in Calabar in which children who were from dysfunctional families joined the streets due to the harsh treatment they were receiving. In line with the social constructivism theory, children's exposure to harmful or uncomfortable home environments leads to an increase in streetism. However, some disagreements exist in which some disjointed families manage to bring children without them leaving for the streets. It is paramount that social workers after assessing the child provide counselling to both the child and the family members and do reunifications or send the child to a place of safety like a children's home until the child is old enough to defend themselves.

According to Ward and Seager (2010), factors such as situations of abuse, domestic violence or poor family relationships are common among street children. Cucumber and Gwegweni (2015), argue that the majority of street children in Africa (70%), were primary school dropouts and some never attended school at all, for reasons that included failure by guardians to pay school fees and buy study materials. Hassen and Manus (2018), also argue that approximately 76% of children did not go to school or were dropouts at primary school in Africa. Cumber and Gwegweni (2015), cite violence and sexual abuse, HIV/AIDS and STIs, substance use/ abuse, and sexual reproductive disorders as constituting some of the challenges street children experience. Salihu (2019), notes that the girl child in the streets of Iran was at high risk of sexual abuse. UNICEF (2001), postulates that younger boys tend to engage in sex with older boys for protection in Zimbabwe

Main source of living

The majority of the street children survive by vending (selling biscuits, sweets, cigarettes, and other items, begging, and shoplifting. Children get their living from mainly vending and begging. They also get some meals, particularly during weekends from Street Ahead. This is in line with ARISE (2001); Mannan, 2004; & Hasan, (1990) who note that harsh realities coerce them to survive on the streets with an array of social exclusions, and push them to work and have food by stealing, begging or other means that are ultimately the result of abandonment of their destiny on the streets. UNICEF (2007), noted that some street children engaged in selling on the roads, railway stations, and highways and some are engaged in petty activities to feed themselves and to meet their other needs. UNODC, (2018), postulates that street children sometimes engage in street vending and hustling to earn a living. Mokomane and Makaoaes (2015) main findings showed that all shelters offer some form of therapeutic, developmental and recreational programs and that they are trying to reach the street children at a preventive level. Children are forced to find survival strategies to survive hence social workers must work with all stakeholders to put these children into a place of safety and then provide skills building to children so that they can provide for themselves when they are old enough.

Challenges encountered in the streets by the children

The major challenges encountered by street children include physical abuse, sexual abuse, hunger, and exposure to diseases. Children in the street experience physical abuse. The streets are not a haven for children yet they left their homes because of abuse among others and they also face the same fate in the streets. Physical abuse for children was found to be high in the streets of Harare. This is in sync with literature which states not only scarcity of family needs or poverty but family problems such as torture of the stepmothers, bigamy of father, mother or father or both parents' death pushed them to the streets (Rahman and Rahman, 2013:54). They experience physical abuses ranged from minor bruises to severe fractures or death as a result of punching, beating, kicking, biting, shaking, throwing, stabbing, choking, hitting with a hand, stick, strap, or another object, and burning by their peers or caregivers or other persons (Hamid and Thampi, 2011; CWIG, 2013; ARISE, 1999). It is paramount that social workers provide counselling and a place of safety for these children.

Sexual abuse was also found to be a prominent challenge that is faced in the streets of Harare. The professional staff revealed that young girls are the most affected population in they are sexually abused by other street children, security guards, and other older men who molest and solicit sexual favours from the young street girls. On the other hand, it was also found that cases of sodomy in the streets exist in which the boys are being sodomized even by older men and their peers. They are prone to sexual abuses like penetration for sexual intercourse or coitus, incest, rape, sodomy, indecent exposure, and exploitation by vagabonds, pedestrians, and other adults (UNICEF, 2007:3; CWIG, 2013). The fact that children are being abused in the streets highlights the need for social workers to advocate for these children to be moved into a place of safety.

Children in the streets survive by begging, vending, and stealing. Children experience extreme hunger because they are not guaranteed meals in the streets. In some cases, they fail to spend the whole day without getting a single meal. It was obtained that children end up eating food from bins which is not safe for human consumption. From the 18 street children who were interviewed, 15 indicated challenges such as brutality and assaults from police and security guards, sexual abuse, and exposure to diseases due to harsh weather conditions.

Street children are exposed to very tough conditions that affect their well-being and developmental milestones. The challenges that children experience in the streets expose the extent to which children are abused and neglected both in their homes and in the streets. No indication of child protection was highlighted during the interviews with the children. On the contrary, the police who should be custodians of children were cited to be the ones exacerbating the abuse of children by beating them and chasing them away exposing the children to more dangers of the streets. Street children managed to get foods either pure or rotten. Almost a half of them could take meals thrice a day but one-fourth reported to take just once (5%) or twice (20%) a day (Rahman, Habibur Rahman, Zakaria &Monjur-Ul-Haide, 2015). They failed to bring changes in the existing survival patterns due to social stigma, negligence and indefinite income sources (Rahman and Rahman, 2013: 55-56).

Interventions and Social Work's Response to Prevent Streetism

The major interventions to prevent streetism include law enforcement, placing street children in places of safety, and making home assessments to protect children who are exposed to harmful home environments. This position concurs with a study by Abrams & Alan (2020) that focused on the voices of frontline workers in which social workers were found to be huge players in responding to the needs of children in harmful home environments as well as harsh conditions in the streets. For example, the chapter has already mentioned how social workers during the COVID-19 era worked hard to place street children in hotel spaces that were leased by the government to maximize the protection of children. Canadian social workers also responded to the calls of children both in homes and on the streets providing the needed psychosocial social support. These social work practices are not foreign to the Zimbabwean situation since organizations have schedules for providing psychosocial support and the provision of other needs such as meals, clothing, and shelter. However, there exists a huge gap on the part of social workers who are failing to offer effective support to promote the well-being of children on the streets and safeguard their rights.

The DSD among other stakeholders mentions resource limitations yet children are still flocking to the streets. It appears social work is forgotten and not known in Zimbabwe in which children do not know which services are provided by social workers and they suffer in silence until they take the wildest decision to live in the streets. Based on the mass exodus of social workers from Zimbabwe to greener pastures such as the UK, USA, Australia, Canada, and Poland among others, social workers in Zimbabwe childcare-related organizations and stakeholders who help street children are increasingly becoming more incapacitated. The incapacitation of these stakeholders implies more sorrow for the street children. The increase in street children in Harare is hard to combat given the challenges that the social work profession, government, and stakeholders are experiencing. Therefore, De brito (2014) writes that organizations should have an involvement in creating a meaningful protection system. According to Nikku (2012), social workers work with children in need and provide services to ensure street children's rights. Thus, social workers should play their role in protecting these children and stakeholders should also work hand in hand with social workers to mitigate this problem.

Recommendations

The following recommendations should be emphasized:

- The Department of Social Development, Council of Social Work, National Association of Social Workers, and other stakeholders that have a direct connection with children should redefine the role of social work in Zimbabwe primarily in reducing the flocking of children into the streets of Harare. The redefinition of social work roles will help improve the safeguarding of children from various forms of abuse.

- Schools, churches, and other groups that directly deal with children should be engaged by the government through training for capacity building to ensure that children are protected and safeguarded from various forms of abuse both in the home environment and or the streets.

- DSD should intensify home visits and assessments through partnerships with related stakeholders to identify children who are at risk of joining street life.

- Law enforcers such as Home Affairs should intensify their operations to protect children in all circles of life rather than causing more harm to street children. This will help in curbing police brutality on street children.

- The government should consider increasing the number of childcare institutions in the country by turning some unused state properties to work as houses of safety such that children living in the streets can be given shelter and places of safety.

- A tour of the streets of Harare is urgently needed by government ministries and other concerned stakeholders to ensure that children are emancipated from the hell of challenges they face in the streets. Urgent measures should be taken by the government to curb child prostitution, the increase in unwanted teenage pregnancies, child trafficking, the spread of STIs, and HIV/AIDS among others.

- The government through other bodies should empower social workers to maximize child protection by providing adequate funding for these professions through their various organizations. Adequate funding to government departments that work with children promotes and enhances the implementation of child protection measures in the country.

Conclusion

The issue of street children has become a problem in Zimbabwe which needs all stakeholders to come up with preventative systems that protect and save the best interest of children. Although many African countries have been affected, it is important that all these countries work hand in hand in trying to mitigate the problem so that we achieve the SGDs and the development of our nations. However, even the few stakeholders that have been trying their best to provide street children with food, it is not effective enough to stop the increase of these children in the streets. Social workers should ensure street children's rights and make sure that social justice prevail.

References

ABRAMS Laura S. and DETTLAFF Alan J., 2020. "Voices from the Frontlines: Social Workers Confront the COVID-19 Pandemic." *Social Work* 65 (3): 302–305.

AMINEH Roya Jafari and DAVATGARI ASL Hanieh, 2015. "Review of Constructivism and Social Constructivism." *Journal of Social Sciences, Literature and Languages* 1 (1): 9–16.

ASHCROFT Rachelle, SUR Deepy, GREENBLATT Andrea and DONAHUE Peter, 2022. "The Impact of the COVID-19 Pandemic on Social Workers at the Frontline: A Survey of Canadian Social Workers." *The British Journal of Social Work* 52 (3): 1724–46.

BAHAR Herwina, HASSAN Zainudin and FIRAS Hanny, 2019. "Overcome the Problem of Street Children through Life Skill Learning in West Java, Indonesia." *Indian Journal of Public Health Research & Development* 10 (4).

COMPASS CHILDREN'S CHARITY, 2023. "Street Children Worldwide." https://compasschildrenscharity.org.uk.

CONSORTIUM FOR STREET CHILDREN, 2018. *Street Children: A Global Picture.* https://childhub.org.

ENDRIS Sofiya, and SITOTA Galata, 2019. "Causes and Consequences of Streetism among Street Children in Harar City, Ethiopia." *International Journal of Education and Literacy Studies* 7 (2): 94–99.

FEKADU Daniel and NIKAPOTA Anula, 2020. "Street Children, Exploitation, and Slavery." In *Mental Health and Illness of Children and Adolescents*, 1–10.

GUNHIDZIRAI C. Constance, 2020. "Implementation of Government Social Protection Programmes in Mitigating the Challenges Faced by Street Children in Zimbabwe." *Gender and Behavior* 18 (3).

KANJANDA Offard and VONGAI CHIPARANGE Getrude, 2015. "Street Kids in the Christian World: A Case of Mutare Urban, Zimbabwe." *European Scientific Journal* 11 (29).

KAWALA Brenda Allen, KIBIWOTT KIRUI Brian and NAMBILE CUMBER Samuel 2020. "Effect of COVID-19 Response in Uganda on Street Children." *The Pan African Medical Journal* 35 (Suppl 2).

MIA Md Tuhin and ISLAM Monirul 2021. "Legal Protection of Street Children in Bangladesh: With References to International and National Laws." *Journal of Asian and African Social Science and Humanities* 7 (2): 34–49.

NDLOVU Everson and TIGERE Richard 2022. "Life in the Streets, Children Speak Out: A Case of Harare Metropolitan, Zimbabwe." *Life* 5 (1): 25–45.

NDULOR Cosmas Ukanwa, 2022. "Street Children Phenomenon: Implication for Nigerian Society." *SIST Journal of Religion and Humanities* 2 (1).

OTIGBA David Somto, 2022. *Social Work with Street Children and Youth in Nigeria.* PhD diss., Mykolo Romerio universitetas.

SHITINDI Jeston, 2023. "Influence of Poverty on Streetism of Children in Dar es Salaam and Dodoma Cities." *Journal of Poverty, Investment and Development* 8 (1): 1–15.

SOHAIL Amir Humza, HASSAAN ARIF MAAN Muhammad and SOHAIL Sachal, 2021. "Sex and the Streets: The Open Secret of Sexual Abuse among Pakistan's Two Million Street Children." *Child and Adolescent Psychiatry and Mental Health* 15 (1): 1–4.

UDUIGWOMEN Godspower Andrew, 2019. "History and Impact of Child Streetism in Calabar, 1943–2015." Unpublished MA Thesis. Department of History and International Studies, University of Calabar.

VAMEGHI Meroe, ROSHANFEKR Payam, GHAEDAMINI HAROUNI Gholamreza, TAKAFFOLI Marzieh and BAHRAMI Giti 2023. "Street Children in Iran: What Are Their Living and Working Conditions? Findings from a Survey in Six Major Cities." *International Journal of Environmental Research and Public Health* 20 (7): 5271.

WEBB Nancy Boyd, 2019. *Social Work Practice with Children.* New York: Guilford Publications.

A Chorus of Voices in Safeguarding: Weaving Children's Stories in Narrative Therapy

Mercy Shumbamhin and Isaac Mutelo

Introduction and Background

Worldwide, nations including African states are increasingly making advances in the area of child safeguarding as part of ensuring that children enjoy their rights as enshrined in the United Nations Convention on the Rights of the Child (UNCRC) (1989). In Africa, the following writers highlight some of the child safeguarding efforts made across the African continent (Chisale 2019; Johnson & Nielsen 2020; Warria & Chikadzi 2020; Daka & Gikonyo 2022). The United Nations Convention on the Rights of the Child (UNCRC) is the most ratified human rights treaty in the world, covering 54 basic rights of a child aged 0-18 (McMellon & MacLachlan 2021). The United Nations Committee on the Rights of the Child has made protecting children's rights to life, dignity, well-being, health, development, participation, and non-discrimination a top concern (MacLachlan, McMellon & Inchley 2022). In Africa, the major instrument calling for the continent to observe children's rights is the African Children's Charter on the Rights and Welfare of the Child (ACRWC) (Murungi 2021). It is worth noting that Zimbabwe has signed both the UNCRC and the ACRWC and that Zimbabwe itself has a Constitution that has sections that relate to child protection and child safeguarding (Magaya & Fambisayi 2021).

No matter the circumstance, every child has the right to be protected from violence, exploitation, and abuse (UNICEF 2023). Safeguarding is the action that is taken to promote the welfare of children and protect them from harm. This includes protecting children from abuse and maltreatment, preventing harm to children's health or development, ensuring children grow up with the provision of safe and effective care, and taking action to enable all children and young people to have the best outcomes. We are all responsible for ensuring our children can grow up free from violence, exploitation and abuse; as parents, caregivers, teachers, health workers, community leaders, religious leaders or government officials (UNICEF 2023). African values and norms encourage everyone to participate in the raising and nurturing of children (Chisale 2019). This resonates with the African proverb which says, "It takes a village to raise a child,". It reflects the communal responsibility for children's well-being. The extended family, which includes grandparents, aunties, uncles, and other family members contribute to safeguarding children's rights.

Despite this cultural wisdom and consideration, children in Africa often suffer from physical abuse, sexual abuse, psychological abuse, emotional abuse or neglect, (Government of Zimbabwe 2001; Muzingili & Taruvinga 2017; Daka & Gikonyo 2022). And yet child abuse is an underreported phenomenon despite its high global prevalence. In child protection literature, there is limited knowledge on how best to protect children. We have known from early childhood theories, research, and practice that children are active constructors of meaning with voices to be heard and the capacity to express their views with wisdom and insight (Shumbamhini 2008). The chapter argued that children are key informants and experts on their own lives and, indeed, are our best source of advice for matters affecting them, including safeguarding issues. Hence, the children are "a chorus of voices" co-creating together in harmony their stories into a beautiful safeguarding document.

Weaving of Children's Stories in Narrative Therapy

Millions of children are confronted with pain and suffering of many children (Cochrane, De Gruchy and Petersen 1991:18). Ethically, this calls one to a commitment to transformation, positioning oneself on the side of the suffering children, against all oppressive or exploitative discussions and practices. Transformation occurs when there is the power of empathy and compassion, of delight in the otherness, and strength in the solidarity of listening to the children's stories, bearing together stories of pain and suffering (Welch 1990:135).

The weaving of children's stories in narrative therapy unveils information related to a child's protection and safeguarding is confined to the stories that children tell. These stories call one to accountability, they invite one to listen to the children's voices concerning their welfare, protection, and safeguarding. The inclusion of children's voices in this chapter therefore necessitates the utilization of suitable approaches in child safeguarding that are capable of empowering children to share their lived experiences and perspectives.

The weaving metaphor symbolises many African cultures that treasure weaving as an art. Weaving is an important part of African culture, and it can be a symbol of identity. The patterns and colours used in African weaving are often symbolic representing the people's history, storytelling, religion and politics (Noda 2018). For example, in the Zimbabwean Shona culture, the mat is a metaphor for connections and unity. These mats are used to communicate ideas, commitment, friendship, respect, devotion, rootedness and belonging. As you weave, you are weaving your life and present community into a rich history of art. You are weaving the future of your community's continued identity (Noda 2018). Each mat tells a story about the culture and history of its people and, in some cases can be used as a historical document (Amatuli Artefacts 2021). This chapter has woven the children's threads or narratives of their own lives into their preferred patterns of safeguarding. Narrative analysis is a qualitative method focused on interpreting human experience in the form of stories or narratives. It focuses on the stories people tell about their experiences. It is a way of understanding how people make sense of their lives and the world around them. Narrative inquiry is based on the premise that people understand and give meaning to their lives through the stories they tell (Andrews et al. 2013). In doing so, people utilize narratives to compose and order their life experiences. Through the use of story forms, people account for and give meaning or significance to their lives (Bleakley 2000).

Connelly and Clandinin (1990) who are among the early proponents of narrative research proposed to put the person back at the centre of research inquiry ensuring that people's voices are not lost in translation. The two main elements comprising this approach are the participants' account of a particular experience and the exploration of meaning embedded in the participants' stories. The focus on particular experiences is from the belief that lives are bounded by events which vary in significance to the people involved. Exploration of personal meaning refers to the fact that meanings are evolving and persons may recognize some meanings and not others.

African Women's Perspective on Child Safeguarding

African women see women's struggle for liberation as liberation for all, men, women, children and societies. They raise their voices against patriarchal, oppressive, and harmful cultural and religious practices that impact child safeguarding. These practices perpetuate gender inequality and contribute to girls and women's suffering. African women critique traditions that perpetuate harmful practices such as forced marriages, female genital mutilation (FGM), child marriage, and virginity testing. These practices often result in abuse, violence and suffering for the girl child. They therefore advocate for stronger laws against child abuse, exploitation, and neglect.

According to (Kasomo & Masemo 2011) African women understand that the well-being of the community and the extended family is one of the key responsibilities accorded to them by their ancestors. In African communities, women have historically played essential roles in procreation, child care, and communal co-existence. They often serve as primary caregivers for children. They provide emotional support, nurture, and create safe environments for children. African women prioritise the significance of family and community by searching for the positive, life-affirming aspects of culture in safeguarding issues. They see child abuse as a result of the weak communal parenting or adult guidance fundamental to African communities (Chisale 2019). The suffering of children in African communities is therefore understood as the community's failure. As a result, African women's perspective criticises structures that perpetuate the suffering of all vulnerable community members, including women, children, the elderly and those who live with disabilities.

African women therefore campaign for the Ubuntu philosophy. They argue that Africans are highly community-oriented and sensitive to the needs of others and the well-being of the whole community especially the vulnerable members (Oduyoye 2001). According to African values, children come into the world utterly dependent on the community for biological survival and consequent development. There is no need for children in African societies to suffer. The African women advocate for the recovery of Ubuntu which seems to be disappearing and overwhelmed by Western existential values. African women therefore argue that every community has a role to play in the fight for justice, peace, healing and the well-being of all (Ackermann 1991:107; Kasomo & Masemo 2011). African women emphasise that addressing issues related to the dehumanization of children requires collective efforts involving challenging harmful stereotypes and prioritising children's well-being and rights. This encourages collaboration among all African networks and structures, not excluding the traditional networks, in the well-being of the children. A healthy community that works together in raising children is noticeable in the state of the children.

As a result, it is important to acknowledge the significance of African women's perspective in understanding social norms, power dynamics, and the safeguarding issues in African communities. An integration of African women's perspectives into child safeguarding mechanisms became vital. Their involvement ensures that gender-sensitive perspectives are considered in child protection legislation.

Inclusion of Children's Voices

Two theoretical premises are important in thinking about including children's voices in research — the concept of the 2013 Zimbabwean Constitution (Government of Zimbabwe, 2013) and the concept of children's rights as expressed in the United Nations Convention on the Rights of the Child (UNCRC) (United Nations General Assembly 1989). Everyone is bound by the collective duty as enshrined in the new Constitution to uphold the rights of children. Sections 19 and 81 in the new Constitution adopted in 2013 spell out the rights of children and the obligation of all the duty bearers. Section 81 of the new Constitution includes the following provisions, "Every child, that is to say every boy and girl under the age of eighteen years, has the right... to be protected from economic and sexual exploitation, from child labour, and maltreatment, neglect or any form of abuse" (Government of Zimbabwe 2013).

Shumbamhini (2005, 2008) has shown that children are capable of making sense of their views and sharing their views on issues concerning them, and as human beings, they are entitled to express these views. Children can be perceived as active, competent, and reflexive constructors of their own worlds, and she has argued that children have a rightful place as social actors capable of influencing societal matters and policies that directly impact them (Shumbamhini 2008). The child is seen as "rich in potential, strong, powerful, competent, and most of all connected to adults and to other children" (Malaguzzi 1993: 10). In other words, children are their own experts whose "voices can be powerful and possibly richer than those adults acting on behalf of children" (Sorin 2003: 31). Wright (2003) has similarly argued that an insider's perspective holds greater value in informing research, practices, and policies.

The second theoretical premise on the importance of considering children's voices comes from the UNCRC (United Nations General Assembly, 1989). Zimbabwe has been a signatory of this international convention since 1990. Article 1 of the UN Convention on the Rights of the Child states that "In all actions concerning children, whether undertaken by public or private social welfare institutions, court of law, administrative authorities or legislative bodies, the best interest of the child shall be a primary consideration" (United Nations General Assembly 1989). Article 12 of the UNCRC gives due recognition to children's rights to have a voice and the capability to express their views in matters that relate to their lives. The formal endorsement of children's rights within the social-political framework of UNCRC has garnered a greater mandate for eradicating the marginalized social status of children and respecting their role as active citizens in society. It recognizes the individual as well as the collective agency of children.

It is the children's legal right to be protected adequately by the courts and in particular by the High Court as their upper guardian Child rights and primary consideration of the best interest of the child. However, this does not dismiss the responsibility of the African child neither is it a creation of a selfish and perpetually childish new crop of Africans as some people like to think. The African Charter on the Rights and Welfare of the Child (ACRWC) article 31 clearly states that every child shall have responsibilities towards his family and society, the State, and other legally recognised communities and the international community. Responsibilities include among many others, working for the cohesion of the family, respecting his/her parents and elders at all times, and assisting them in case of need. It is, therefore, a primary consideration to see the African child rising above all the challenges the continent may be facing and become an epitome of strength and resilience celebrated and protected by the State, parents and guardians; and all those involved in his or her welfare.

With a strong conviction driven by these theoretical underpinnings, it can be noted that the importance of research *with* children such as listening to their voices does not become merely tokenistic (Dockett, Einarsdottir, & Perry 2011; Shumbamhini 2008). It is therefore imperative for the children to participate in matters that concern them especially sensitive issues such as safeguarding.

Children's Stories

One of the aims of narrative therapy involves a focus on the 'story' and the effects of telling particular stories, in particular ways, in particular contexts (White 2001). Phiri, Govinden & Nadar (2002) hold that telling stories is therapeutic and the process of narrative therapy is crucial in healing and wholeness. Stories can help us find ways forward – transforming our society into one that values the humanity of all people. Story-telling is a very powerful methodology for seeking and co-

constructing alternative stories that enrich children's lives. It is noteworthy that due to limited space, the stories provided here are not the full stories of the children. The four children participants chose their pseudonyms and what they wanted to be included in the chapter. Anna's story is as follows:

> I am a 12-year-old girl and am in Grade Seven, After the death of both our parents, my young brother and myself were put in the care of my aunt. My parents had an accident and they died on the spot. By then, I was 9 years old and my brother was 6 years old. We were never consulted. All our parents' property was taken by my father's brothers. We had to change schools from a boarding school to a day school. I was then sexually abused by my uncle. This affected my well-being. I became both emotionally and physically sick. I could not sleep at all. I was so scared of men. FEAR crippled me. I told my class teacher who then referred me to a social worker. My brother and I were both moved to a place of safety. For me, I think our society or extended families ignore our feelings and views. As children we are often seen but not heard; expected to be silent, obedient, do as we are told and not to think creatively, and expressively, and to take responsibility for our own decisions. It is very important to ask us for example if we are comfortable staying with this uncle or relative even more important to do follow-ups to see how we are coping in this new environment, this is the kind of caring and safeguarding needed for vulnerable children like me and my brother. Instead, people choose to ask the perpetrator not the children, this is not helpful to us, please ask us, we are humans, and we will tell you what is really going on! Safeguarding is everyone's responsibility including children, we have to take care of each other. EVERY CHILD MATTERS! We need education on our rights, personal safety and how to report abuse. There must be suggestion boxes everywhere to report abuse. It is very difficult sometimes in our families to talk about abuse especially for orphaned children. Please create platforms for children to report abuse. It is important that members of the extended family have education on safeguarding. Our government should try to engage the families and communities in the promotion of child safety and well-being. Please encourage open and honest communication with children and **LISTEN TO OUR CONCERNS!** And remember that issues such as inheritance, separation from parents, alternative care, basic education for vulnerable children, and supporting children living with HIV, it is necessary to consult the children and hear our views.

Tatenda's story is as follows:

> I am a boy aged 8. My parents are in the United Kingdom; they went there two years ago. They left me in the care of my maternal grandparents. I live together with my uncle (brother of my mother) who is 19 years old. He abused me on several occasions and I reported this to my grandparents and they said I should not talk about it because he would be imprisoned. I then developed some pain and could not walk properly, I told my friend and my friend's mother brought me to a clinic. My uncle was arrested and my grandparents were very angry with me. I was then taken to a place of safety. I told the therapist that I would like to go to my parents. I am very happy to join my parents next month. My parents thought I was safe with my grandparents and uncle, yet I was not safe at all. I was lonely, suffering, and in great pain. These people were not caring for me but hurting and harming me. I wish my parents did not trust them. They caused me a lot of pain. I had wounds and I was bleeding with nobody caring for me. Nobody heard my cry. They never allowed me to talk to my parents alone, I had to speak to my parents in their presence. I always wanted to whisper to my parents and tell them, I was sick and full of pain in my body. Below is my message to all parents.

> Oh Parents, Parents do not trust anyone, to take care of your children, take them with you wherever you are.

> Oh Parents, Parents buy your children a phone so that you can speak to them directly.

> Oh Parents, Parents ask your child's friend how your child is doing.

> Oh Parents, Parents, ask your child's teacher how your child is doing at school.

> Oh Parents, Parents ask your pastor if your child is coming to church.

> Oh Parents, Parents ask someone to visit your children when you are not there.

> Oh Parents, Parents tell God to look after your children.

Chipo's story is as follows:

> I am 17 years old, and I live with my aunt and my other 3 siblings. My mother is mentally challenged and my father is somewhere in South Africa. He never cared for us. When my mother was ill, he just abandoned all of us at my aunt's place. Our school fees were paid by a donor. We also received food from the same organisation. I have been sexually exploited by an officer from this organisation so that we could get more food and other favours. This did not give me peace of mind and it affected my school performance. Unfortunately, my aunt

seemed to like it because she also got some favours from this officer. The officer told my aunt that he would marry me after my secondary education. I did not love him and I will never love or like someone who abuses his power. Because of poverty and being a child, I became more vulnerable to exploitation and abuse. I was powerless. The officer used his position and power to influence my aunt and control the resources. He would call my aunt Mother and other people thought all was well. There was a power imbalance. Thanks to my teachers who referred me to a therapist. The organisation wanted to deal with this issue as an internal matter, it was afraid of its donor partner but this did not stop me from seeking justice and to fight for my right to be respected and to be treated with dignity. My recommendations to all organisations are that, please have some good practices for safeguarding children at your organisations. You should not just have policies and procedures in place, but take a step further in implementing them and have a background check on your staff. It is important for your organisations to provide support to survivors of abuse. Say **NO TO CHILD ABUSE** and take steps to strengthen accountability in relation to safeguarding by establishing an independent safeguarding committee at your organisation where children could be free to raise their concerns regarding safeguarding.

Finally, Beauty's story is as follows:

I am 15 years old. My mother separated from my father and she remarried. I stay with my father and stepmother. I have been sexually assaulted by my History teacher. He lured me to his office and fondled me. He forced himself on me whilst I tried to pull off. And he threatened to report me to my stepmother who is a teacher at the same school. He said he would tell her that I did not do my schoolwork. I felt helpless and powerless but in the end, I managed to bite his finger hard and he released me. I went and told the deputy head who is always friendly to learners. I am very grateful to her, she reported the case to the police. The teacher was arrested and it was then discovered that I was not the only one. The teacher had sexually assaulted 3 other girls at the same school but the headmaster who was his best friend always swept these cases under the carpet to protect the image of the school at the expense of the learners.

I want to suggest that every school must have Child Rights, Responsibilities, Anti-corruption and Bribery Clubs which will educate both learners and teachers, on equal rights as individuals, no matter how small we are as kids. Nothing for us without us. Please empower not only teachers but also learners to lead these clubs. Some of the teachers are real wolves, they are there to destroy us. We have the right to be respected and to voice our opinions on our education and concerns, working with our teachers to inform and direct our education and environment. We deserve to be given and take responsibility for our own situation and futures and to be respected and valued for this, as active participants within our communities. Just remember, we are the future and leaders of tomorrow. Please take care and protect your future generations.

Narrative therapy with children

Narrative therapy is a respectful, non-judgmental and collaborative approach to therapy that focuses on the stories people tell about themselves and their lives (Morgan 2000). It helps children and families to externalize their problems, identify their strengths, and create new narratives that empower them. In narrative therapy, problems are viewed as dominant stories influenced by cultural, social, historical, and political contexts, and the goal is to facilitate the individual in replacing thin, problem-oriented stories with preferred thickened narratives about their personal lives. The problem addressed by the individual is not viewed as a dysfunction, but as a story that needs to be reconstructed through therapeutic conversations and practices. Through these conversations, people become agents in their own lives by describing everyday situations in words that reflect their unique experiences (White 1988).

According to White and Morgan (2006) narrative therapy with children involves creating a safe and playful environment where children can share their stories through various mediums such as art, drama, and play activities. This allows children to tell their stories in a way that makes sense to them, and for more detailed descriptions to emerge (White, 2007). In this sense, the conversation can become more inviting for the child, enabling them to talk about concerns and what is important to them without pressuring the child to express himself exclusively through language. Consequentially, this may allow the child more direct access to overlooked aspects of their life such as safeguarding and to see problems from different perspectives and through new constructions of narratives (White 2007).

Narrative therapy is very useful in therapeutic work with children because it is flexible and encourages the child to look at life moments in which the problem was not around, exploring celebrations and achievements, an opportunity for the child to begin rewriting their story without the problem. According to Mergle (2015), it can be particularly effective for children who have experienced trauma, abuse, or other life-altering events. It can help children to develop a sense of agency, build resilience, and cope with difficult emotions. The therapist acts as a facilitator who listens actively and asks open-ended questions that help the child to re-author their story in a way that is more positive and hopeful (Mergle 2015).

Narrative Techniques that are Effective in Therapy

Externalizing Conversations

Externalizing, or separating the person from his or her problem-saturated story, is a central approach in narrative therapy. According to Freedman and Combs (2004:142) externalisation is a practice supported by the belief that a problem is something operating on, impacting, or pervading a person's life, something separate and different from the person". Externalizing conversations can help challenge self-destructive beliefs and behaviours. By engaging in therapeutic externalizing conversations, it is possible to re-author one's life, challenge dominant knowledge and social practices, and develop a preferred alternative narrative. In the context of children, externalizing conversations can be used to help them understand that their problems are not an inherent part of their identity (Morgan 2000). Instead, they are separate from them and can be addressed as such. This can be especially helpful for children who may feel overwhelmed or powerless in the face of their problems.

Narrative therapists are interested in engaging in a conversation to situate the problem away from people who consult them. Thus, when the participating children tell their stories, they listen for the word(s) that affect them. For example, a child might say, "I just get so worried about my future that I can't sleep at night". In this case, a narrative therapist picks up on the word 'worry' and say, "So the Worry is stopping you from sleeping at night?".

Externalising conversations enabled me to be a part of the process of children reclaiming their lives from the effects of problems affecting them. Externalizing language separated children from their problems and created a lighter atmosphere wherein children saw themselves as separate from the problem. They no longer felt guilt about what happened to them. Externalising conversations disempowered the effects of the problems which were affecting the children such as worry, blame, guilt, and shame (White 1991:29).

Drawing narrative therapy

Telling our stories transforms children's lives and drawing narrative therapy is a way of telling their stories. Drawing narrative therapy is a therapeutic technique that uses art to help clients process and heal from trauma. Research in art therapy has shown that drawings enable the expression of hidden or repressed thoughts and feelings in a relatively fast and straightforward way (Woolford et al. 2013). Drawing helps the children to reconnect and integrate fragmented memories, express emotions, and gain new perspectives on their lives. When words are not enough, they turn to images and symbols to tell their stories. In telling their stories through drawing, they can often find a path to health and wellness, emotional repair, recovery, and, ultimately, transformation (Boden et al., 2019). Drawing helps individuals explore and express their thoughts and feelings (Harpaz 2014). Drawing was a very powerful tool in narrative therapy because it helped the children externalize their problems and create new stories about their lives. Drawing helped me as the therapist by shedding light on the children's internal and outer world as well as their perception of safeguarding issues. Drawing communicated their feelings and ideas of the environment.

Digital narrative therapy

Digital narrative therapy is a form of narrative therapy that uses digital media to help people tell their stories. It can include a wide range of digital gadgets such as videos, photos, and audio recordings (Cohen et al 2015). In this digital era, digital narrative therapy is very powerful in helping people to communicate their stories, even if it is simply by finding and identifying with digital images or stories found on the web. Digital storytelling can help people process traumatic experiences or difficult emotions by allowing them to express themselves creatively. Digital narrative therapy is a very powerful tool for healing and growth. It helps children develop new narratives about themselves that are more positive and empowering. It is important to note that, Amanda Todd was a 15-year-old teenager who committed suicide after posting a video on YouTube in which she used a series of flash cards to tell of her experience of being cyber-bullied through the social networking website Facebook (Todd 2012). People around the world continue to react to the death of this teenage girl who chose a popular tool to communicate her despair. Her decision to end her life, after sharing her story, highlights the urgent need for families, schools, and institutions to take proactive measures to equip children/ students in need with tools that may prevent such tragedies.

Amanda Todd's story is a tragic example of a child who may not have had the support to rewrite her narrative in such a way that she would have been able to empower herself. It is therefore important for therapists and counsellors to offer children and students a variety of digital tools which can help them in times of distress or traumatic experiences (Smith 2008).

Re-authoring narrative therapy

Re-authoring narrative therapy is a process in which a narrative therapist helps people challenge their stories and encourages them to consider alternative stories. Re-authoring conversations take place between a therapist and the person(s) who have come to see them and involve the identification and co-creation of alternative storylines of identity. According to Epston (1998:24-25):

> A re-authoring therapy intends to assist persons in resolving problems by: (1) enabling them to separate their lives and relationships from knowledges/stories that are impoverishing; (2) assisting them to challenge practices of self and relationship that are subjugating; and (3) encouraging persons to re-author their lives according to alternative knowledges/stories and practices of self and relationship that have preferred outcomes.

According to White (2007), "effective therapy is about engaging people in the re-authoring of the compelling plights of their lives in ways that arouse curiosity about human possibility and in ways that invoke the play of imaginations". The process of clients re-authoring their lives involves noticing the "quiet," unnoticed stories that can support clients' budding identities as they separate themselves from their problems (Walter 2018). As a narrative therapist listens to the children's stories, he or she might notice the events that contradict the dominant story, which are known as unique outcomes (Morgan 2000:52), or "sparkling moments" (Freedman & Combs 1996:89; Russell & Carey 2004:23). In other words, one listens for the times when the problem had less or no influence. In some cases, re-authoring conversations are used to help the children rewrite their story in a way that emphasizes their strengths and abilities, rather than focusing on their problems.

Narrative therapeutic letters

Narrative therapeutic letters have been used widely as a contribution to the therapeutic process, as captured in the work of Michael White and David Epston the founders of Narrative Therapy. Narrative letters can be used as potent records of therapeutic conversation to underline and consolidate what has been discovered in therapy. They acknowledge and engage, building on the therapeutic relationship (Moules 2003) and the impact of the therapeutic conversation (Nylund & Thomas 1994). Narrative therapeutic letters are a form of narrative therapy that can be used to help children who have experienced trauma. These letters are written by therapists and are designed to help children understand their experiences and develop new, more positive narratives about themselves. The letters can be used to help children explore their feelings, thoughts, and behaviours in a safe and supportive environment.

Narrative therapists meet with children and families experiencing psychological trauma from abuse by a trusted family member. Time is precious and yet there can be many matters the family wishes for us to talk about. One of my intentions in writing therapeutic letters to the people we meet with is to ensure every moment we have together counts. Writing a letter allows discoveries and meanings to be remembered and potentiated through recipients reading and re-reading a letter. Families do appreciate these letters because they find them encouraging and empowering. Narrative therapeutic letters are useful tools for consolidating emerging alternative narratives about children's lives and help to position children as witnesses to their own abilities or values which have been forgotten or concealed as a consequence of trauma. The reciprocity of the letter-writing process also allows for mutual trust and respect to develop, enhancing the therapeutic relationship (Bjoroy et al 2016).

Writing a letter following the completion of a therapeutic assessment report is an opportunity to share our emerging understandings of the child and their story directly with them (Pyle 2020). Writing letters to children creates an opportunity to provide the child with an experience of being seen, understood and accepted. Therapeutic letters communicate to the children that understand their needs, feelings, and aspirations.

Conclusion

This chapter has shown that involving children's voices in research is crucial for several reasons. Firstly, it is a fundamental right of children to have their voices heard and their opinions taken into account in matters that affect them such as safeguarding. Secondly, children's perspectives can provide valuable insights into their experiences and needs, which can help researchers and policymakers develop more effective interventions and safeguarding policies. Thirdly, involving children in research can help empower them and build their confidence and self-esteem. Finally, it can help to foster positive relationships between children and adults, which can be beneficial to both parties in our African communities. The chapter has also shown that narrative therapy is collaborative, respectful, strength-based, non-judgemental, non-threatening (Shumbamhini 2022) and even playful- child-centred in its approach to dealing with problems, which makes it particularly suited for children in the African context. On that basis, safeguarding is everyone's responsibility, and so children, government, agencies, families, schools, communities, and professionals should work together to safeguard and promote children's welfare and protect them from harm.

References

ACKERMANN Denise, 1991. "Postscript by a Feminist Practical Theologian." In *In Word and Deed: Towards a Practical Theology for Social Transformation*, edited by J. R. Cochrane, J. W. De Gruchy, and R. Peterson, 106–11. Pietermaritzburg: Cluster Publications.

AMATULI ARTEFACTS, 2021. *Woven Together: The Art of African Weaving.* Accessed October 21, 2023.

ANDREWS Molly, SQUIRE Corinne and TAMBOUKOU Maria, eds. 2013. *Doing Narrative Research*. London: Sage.

BLEAKLEY Alan, 2000. "Writing with Invisible Ink: Narrative, Confessionalism, and Reflective Practice." *Reflective Practice* 1 (1): 11–24.

BJORØY Anja, MADIGAN Stephen and NYLAND David, 2016. "The Practice of Therapeutic Letter Writing in Narrative Therapy." In *The Handbook of Counselling Psychology*. London: Sage.

BODEN Zoë, LARKIN Michael and IYERC Malvika, 2019. "Picturing Ourselves in the World: Drawings, Interpretative Phenomenological Analysis, and the Relational Mapping Interview." *Qualitative Research in Psychology* 16: 218–36. https://doi.org/10.1080/14780887.2018.1540679.

CHISALE Sinenhlanhla, 2019. "An Integrated African Pastoral Care Approach to Unaccompanied Refugee Minors Based on Verryn's Child Interventions." ResearchGate. Accessed November 5, 2023.

CHRISTENSEN Pia and JAMES Allison, eds. 2008. *Research with Children: Perspectives and Practices*. 2nd ed. London: Routledge.

CLANDININ Jean and CONNELLY Michael, 1991. "Narrative and Story in Practice and Research." In *The Reflective Turn: Case Studies in and on Educational Practice*, edited by Donald A. Schön, 258–81. New York: Teachers College Press.

COHEN Joshua, JOHNSON Lauren and ORR Penny, 2015. *Video and Filmmaking as Psychotherapy Research and Practice.* Accessed October 24, 2023. https://scholar.google.com.

COCHRANE James, DE GRUCHY John and PETERSEN Robin, eds. 1991. *In Word and Deed: Towards a Practical Theology for Social Transformation.* Pietermaritzburg: Cluster Publications.

CONNELLY Michael and CLANDININ Jean Clandinin. 1990. "Stories of Experience and Narrative Inquiry." *Educational Researcher* 19 (5): 2–14.

DAKA Lawrence and GIKONYO Beatrice, 2022. *Creating a Consistent Culture of Safeguarding in Church and Society: Perspective from Africa.* Jesuit Conference of Africa and Madagascar.

DENZIN Norman and LINCOLN Yvonna, 1994. "Introduction: Entering the Field of Qualitative Research." In *Handbook of Qualitative Research*, edited by Norman Denzin and Yvonna Lincoln. London: Sage.

DOCKETT Susan, EINARSDOTTIR Johanna and PERRY Bob, 2011. "Balancing Methodologies and Methods in Researching with Young Children." In *Researching Young Children's Perspectives: Debating the Ethics and Dilemmas of Educational Research with Children*, edited by Deborah Harcourt, Bob Perry, and Tim Waller, 68–81. Oxon: Routledge.

EPSTON David. 1998. *Catching Up with David Epston: A Collection of Narrative Practice-Based Papers Published between 1991 and 1996*. Adelaide: Dulwich Centre Publications.

FREEDMAN Jill and COMBS Gene, 1996. *Narrative Therapy: The Social Construction of Preferred Realities*. New York: Norton.

___, 2004. "A Poststructuralist Approach to Narrative Work." In *The Handbook of Narrative and Psychotherapy: Practice, Theory and Research*, edited by Lynne E. Angus and John McLeod, 200–14. Thousand Oaks: Sage.

GAVENTA John and CORNWALL Andrea, 2001. "Power and Knowledge." In *Handbook of Action Research: Participative Inquiry and Practice*, edited by Peter Reason and Hilary Bradbury, 70–80. London: Sage.

GOVERNMENT OF ZIMBABWE, 2001. *Children's Act (Chapter 5:06)*. Harare: Government Printers.

___, 2013. *Constitution of Zimbabwe Amendment Number 20*. Harare: Government Printers.

GREENE Shiela and HOGAN Diane, eds. 2005. *Researching Children's Experience: Methods and Approaches*. London: Sage.

HALLETT Christine and PROUT Alan, 2003. *Hearing the Voices of Children in Social Policy*. Oxon: Routledge.

HARPAZ Ruth, 2014. *Document*. Accessed October 21, 2023. https://shs.hal.science/halshs-01081464.

JOHNSON Afrooz and NIELSEN Julia, 2020. *Child Protection, Safeguarding and the Role of the African Charter on the Rights and Welfare of the Child*. Accessed October 27, 2023. https://scielo.org.za.

KASOMO Daniel and MASENO Loreen, 2011. "A Critical Appraisal of African Feminist Theology." *International Journal of Current Research* 2 (1): 154–62.

MAGAYA Isabel and RONGEDZAYI Fambisayi, 2021. "Giant Leaps or Baby Steps? A Preliminary Review of the Development of Children's Rights Jurisprudence in Zimbabwe." *De Jure Law Journal* 54 (1): 1–8.

MACLACHLAN Alice, MCMELLON Christina and INCHLEY Johanna, 2022. "Public Mental Health during the COVID-19 Pandemic: Impacts on Children's Rights." *The International Journal of Human Rights* 29 (4): 10–19.

MALAGUZZI Loris, 1993. "For an Education Based on Relationships." *Young Children* 49 (1): 9–12.

MCMELLON Christina and MACLACHLAN Alice, 2021. "Young People's Rights and Mental Health during Pandemic: An Analysis of the Impact of Emergency Legislation in Scotland." *Sage Open Access* 29 (4): 10–19.

McTAGGART Robin, ed. 1997. *Participatory Action Research: International Contexts and Consequences.* Albany: State University of New York Press.

MERGLER Janine, 2015. *Narrative Therapy for Kids.* Accessed October 20, 2023. https://familiesmagazine.com.au.

MORGAN Alice, 2000. *What Is Narrative Therapy? An Easy-to-Read Introduction.* Adelaide: Dulwich Centre Publications.

MOULES Nancy, 2003. "Therapy on Paper: Therapeutic Letters and the Tone of Relationship." *Journal of Systemic Therapies* 22: 33–49.

MUZINGILI Taruvinga and TARUVINGA Raymond, 2017. "Culturally-Inflected Child Rights Violation." *Journal of Africa Studies* 17 (1). https://www.ajol.info/index.php/mjas/article/view/160926/150491.

NODA Mayu, 2018. "The Art of Weaving in Africa." Accessed October 21, 2023. https://rightforeducation.org/2018/01/29/the-art-of-weaving-in-africa/.

NYLUND David and THOMAS John, 1994. "The Economics of Narrative." *Family Therapy Networker* 18 (6): 38–39.

ODUYOYE Mercy, 2001. *Introducing African Women's Theology.* Sheffield: Sheffield Academic Press.

PHIRI Isabel, GOVINDEN Devarakshanam and NADAR Sarojini, eds. 2002. *Her-Stories: Hidden Histories of Women of Faith in Africa.* Pietermaritzburg: Cluster Publications.

PYLE Laura, 2020. "Yours Truly: Incorporating Therapeutic Letters into the Assessment Process with Children and Young People." Accessed October 22, 2023. https://professionals.childhood.org.au/prosody/2020/07/yours-truly-incorporating-therapeutic-letters-into-the-assessment-process-with-children-and-young-people/.

RUSSELL Shona and CAREY Maggie, 2004. *Narrative Therapy: Responding to Your Questions.* Adelaide: Dulwich Centre Publications.

SHUMBAMHINI Mercy, 2005. "Mary Ward Children's Home: Making the Impossible Become a Reality." *Worldwide Magazine* 15 (3).

___, 2008. *Narrative and Participatory Pastoral Care and Therapy with Children.* DudweilerLandstr: Lambert Academic Publishing.

___, 2022. "Religio-Cultural Norms Constraining Sexual Reproductive Health and Rights for Widows in Zimbabwe." In *Religion, Women's Health Rights, and Sustainable Development in Zimbabwe: Volume 1*, edited by S. Chirongoma, M. Manyonganise, and E. Chitando, 193–211. Cham: Palgrave Macmillan.

SMITH Mark, 2008. "Howard Gardner and Multiple Intelligences." *The Encyclopedia of Informal Education.* Accessed October 25, 2023. http://www.infed.org/mobi/howard-gardner-multiple-intelligences-and-education.

SORIN Reesa, 2003. "Research with Children: A Rich Glimpse into the World of Childhood." *Australian Journal of Early Childhood* 28 (10): 31–35.

THOMSON Pat, 2008. *Doing Visual Research with Children and Young People.* Oxon: Routledge.

TODD Amanda, 2012. "Amanda Todd's Story: Struggling, Bullying, Suicide, Self-Harm." ChiaVideo, October 11. Accessed October 22, 2023.

UNICEF ZIMBABWE, 2023. "Child Protection: Let Children Grow Up Safely!" Accessed October 19, 2023. https://www.unicef.org/zimbabwe.

UNITED NATIONS GENERAL ASSEMBLY, 1989. *Convention on the Rights of the Child.* United Nations Treaty Series, vol. 1577, p. 3. Accessed October 25, 2023. https://www.refworld.org/docid/3ae6b38f0.html.

WALTER Rivera, 2018. "Maps of Narrative Practice: An Overview of Externalizing and Re-Authoring Conversations." *Family Therapy Basics.* Accessed October 22, 2023.

WARRIA Ajwang and CHIKADZI Victor 2020. "The Role of Indigenous Social Protection in Protecting Children: Lessons from Africa." ResearchGate. Accessed October 11, 2023.

WELCH Sharon, 1990. *A Feminist Ethic of Risk.* Minneapolis: Fortress Press.

WHITE Michael, 1988. "Saying Hullo Again: The Incorporation of the Lost Relationship in the Resolution of Grief." *Dulwich Centre Newsletter* 3: 7–11.

___, 1991. "Deconstruction and Therapy." *Dulwich Centre Newsletter* 3: 21–40.

___, 2001. "The Narrative Metaphor in Family Therapy." In *Family Therapy: Exploring the Field's Past, Present and Possible Futures*, edited by David Denborough. Adelaide: Dulwich Centre Publications.

___, 2007. *Maps of Narrative Practice.* New York: Norton.

WHITE Michael, and MORGAN Alice 2006. *Narrative Therapy with Children and Their Families.* Adelaide: Dulwich Centre Publications.

WOOLFORD, Junie, PATTERSON Tess, MACLEOD Emily, HOBBS Linda and HAYNE Harlenr, 2013. "Drawing Helps Children to Talk About Their Presenting Problems During a Mental Health Assessment." *Clinical Child Psychology and Psychiatry* 20: 1–16.

WOODHEAD Martin, and FAULKNER Dorothy 2000. "Subjects, Objects or Participants? Dilemmas of Psychological Research with Children." In *Research with Children: Perspectives and Practices*, edited by Pia Christensen and Allison James, 10–39. London: Falmer Press.

WRIGHT Susan, 2003. *Children, Meaning-Making and the Arts.* NSW, Australia: Pearson Education.

Safeguarding Respect and Opportunities: Lessons from Policies on Children's Work and Child Sexual Abuse.

Michael Bourdillon

Introduction

In July 2023, The British Broadcasting Corporation (BBC) published a report describing how some children in Ghana were violently taken away from their families and had their lives disrupted under the guise of rescuing them from trafficking for child labour (Francavilla, Afreh-Nuamah, and Boateng 2023). It is easy to blame the missionary organisation behind the operation (as did several of the comments on the Youtube page - BBC 2023); but such 'rescue' operations had support among officials and protection services within Ghana. This chapter is about safeguarding children from operations that aim to protect them but turn out to do more damage than they prevent. It is about paying attention to what children need to develop in their different environments.

Psychological studies have shown that in the choices people make consideration of risk frequently focuses on a single danger and overrides a balanced and rational weighing of benefits against costs (Kahnerman 2011). The instinct to protect children from a specific danger therefore easily overshadows consideration of their positive needs, with the result that attempts to protect children from abuse too often result in depriving children of much-needed opportunities to improve their lives, even to the extent of disrupting their lives. The chapter employs studies of children's work and labour and of protection against sexual abuse to illustrate a more general problem in well-intentioned attempts to protect children from harm, and suggest ways forward that are applicable to African contexts.

Children's Work and Labour

Children needing income

My first face-to-face meeting with working children was with an organisation trying to help children living and working on the streets of Harare (Bourdillon 1994; Mapedzahama and Bourdillon 2000). These children showed me new ways of seeing the social world we live in, things that are not easy to understand by someone like me who, after a privileged childhood, lived in elite academic circles. The elite values that I had grown up with did not always work so well for children struggling to survive, who valued what independence they could acquire after the adult world had let them down, sometimes together with their deprived families. For these children, earning money was critical for survival, as well as sometimes providing a chance for positive action and self-respect. When our organisation tried to find less hazardous and more reliable ways of earning for the children, we were criticised for supporting 'child labour'.

There are also cases of children struggling to survive in the rural areas, supporting themselves and their families through work. A teenage girl who became the leader of a group of children involved in artisanal underground mining commented on how their life had improved as a result of this work: there was always money for school fees and for life-supporting medicines (Bourdillon and Musvosvi 2014; Okyere 2014). Ideals of childhood that lie behind much literature and official policy largely derive from the well-resourced societies in which influential people live. Since these ideals reflect the lives of elites, they easily become the goal for others to aim at, sometimes with results that serve the children badly. On the other hand, the lives of poorer children are often challenging: a classic study of children in rural Tonga society of the Zambezi Valley pointed to their heavy workloads, which were often taken for granted rather than being recognised as problematic by the Tonga adults (Reynolds 1991). It seemed appropriate to pay attention to a wider variety of children's work in Zimbabwe. A collection of essays showed children struggling with the work they had to do; but it also showed some children benefitting from their work, sometimes acquiring skills that would help them in adulthood (Bourdillon 2000).

In some parts of Zimbabwe, pupils are contracted to work on estates for an income that covers their school and living expenses and provides a surplus (Bourdillon 1999; Bourdillon 2016). While the treatment of children at such schools can be criticised, some children might wish to be allowed to continue in the scheme – the scheme provides them with better chances for education than was otherwise available to most of them. In 2013, the company running one such estate closed the scheme under pressure from activists against 'child labour'. The closure was declared by some as a "triumph for child rights"; but this "triumph" resulted in some children having to rely on less secure and more poorly paid work that excluded the possibility of schooling (Shumba 2015). There is a problem when well-intentioned efforts to protect children from commercial exploitation end up depriving underprivileged children of an opportunity to improve their lives and driving them into more severe poverty. There is a problem when the principle of abolishing child labour is deemed more important than the damage this policy sometimes does to children's lives. We need to safeguard children's opportunities to benefit from appropriate work and respect them for their efforts.

Romantic Western Ideas vs. Children's Realities

The campaign in Europe to protect children from abusive labour goes back more than two hundred years, fuelled by the hardship, and in some cases serious physical harm, suffered by children forced to work in growing industries. This was contrasted with Romantic notions of childhood as a time for play and learning, without the cares and responsibilities of the adult world, which provides all that the children need. A tendency to contrast work with a good childhood is reinforced in the modern world by visual documentation of extreme work situations, in contrast to lives of idle play and the provision of schooling available to children in well-resourced families. Work for children is easily depicted as "backward", and in opposition to quality schooling that can prepare children for success in the modern world.

The situation of large numbers of children in Africa reveals the inadequacy of this simplistic contrast.[16] Not all work is harmful to children: their work includes a variety of activities that are part of participation in and responsibility for family and community life. Not all schools offer opportunities for a better life to all children: some schools are poor in resources and some pupils struggle with schoolwork. Although schooling does occasionally provide a child from a poor

---

[16] When I started focussing my research on children's work over twenty years ago, a common response from African colleagues was that this was a Western problem, and the negative view on children's work was a Western imposition. Now awareness of abusive work in Africa is more widespread, and Western definitions of, and negative attitudes to, child labour are often accepted as "progressive".

background an education that leads to a more prosperous life, long-term research has shown that school performance relates to the home background more strongly than to any other variables (for example, Murray 2014), and, especially in societies where opportunities for later employment are scarce, schools are weak providers of upward mobility. Besides, very many families in Africa do not have the resources to provide all that the children need without some contribution from the children themselves. Even when families, and the children themselves, recognise work as hazardous and wish for a radical improvement in the lives and chances of the children, they do not wish for an outright ban on children's work, which would likely make their situation worse rather than better (Wouango 2015).

To understand what is best in the situations of the majority of children in the real world, we need a more nuanced view of the benefits and costs of different kinds of work and available schools. Rather than trying to ban work, a more constructive approach to protecting children from exploitation and abusive work involves recognising children as young people trying to find their way in life and growing in responsibility for themselves and their families and communities. As is obvious to most people brought up in African cultures (and indeed most cultures in the world) responsible work is a normal part of life and a gradual introduction to work is beneficial to developing children. From an early age, children participate in work activities, playfully at first, but more constructively as they acquire competence. Through work, they establish themselves as responsible family and community members and acquire technical and social skills that can help them later in life (Bourdillon 2017). Nevertheless, there are risks that work can be exploitative, and that it can be dangerous in ways that people often do not notice immediately. As in other activities of children (including sports), risks can be minimised and weighed against the potential benefits of the activity. Where work is beneficial to children, they need protection *in* their work, which is not the same as protection *from* work.

Recent research in Canada looked at safety issues in paid work of children aged 10 to 16 years (Raby and Sheppard 2023). In Canadian society, such work is widely taken for granted rather than being perceived as problematic "child labour", which is how many would likely perceive it if it took place in poorer communities. There has been some concern, however, at increasing accidents involving children at work, with suggestions that the way to prevent injury to children is to establish a minimum age under which employment should be banned. The research revealed that children were often unaware of risks arising in apparently safe work: these included injury from unsafe machinery, accidents that could be prevented by reasonable attention to safety standards and safety training, and relational problems including sexual harassment. There are ways of reducing risks to working children without removing the development opportunities that appropriate work can provide.

"Work" vs "labour"

Some people have tried to distinguish between "child work", which is beneficial to children or at least not harmful, and "child labour", which is defined as in some way harmful to children. This distinction appears to work well enough in extreme cases: some light tasks are not in any way harmful to children; in contrast, long hours in dangerous work leaving little or no time for schooling or leisure is harmful and unacceptable. However, much work has potential for both benefits and harm, depending on the competencies and training of the particular children, on the conditions under which they work, and especially on the human relations surrounding it. Even to establish risks of harm does not mean that children are harmed. The human mind is attracted to the order created by dividing activities into such clear categories as "good" and "harmful"; the real world, however, is less tidy with good and bad mixed in ways that are lost in such categorisation. To assess whether the net harm in a particular job outweighs its benefits, we need to take into account the context in which it is performed as well as the holistic context of the children's lives – what realistically are the alternatives available to them?[17]

Work and school

Children's work is frequently depicted as opposed to education therefore hindering children's development. This appears to be supported by widespread inverse correlations between work on the one hand and school achievement on the other: taking broad averages, the more work children do, the less well they are likely to do at school and the sooner they are likely to drop out. People often assume from this that work either excludes school or reduces school achievement. Again, careful analysis of the real lives of children reveals a more complex situation. Certainly, many children are compelled, or sometimes choose, to work so much that they have insufficient time and energy for schoolwork; such situations are unacceptable. Even in such cases, however, as the case of the earn-and-learn schools illustrates, the work may make schooling possible. Further,

---

[17] For a full discussion, see Bourdillon et al. 2010; a summary of the principal argument is freely available in Bourdillon 2009.

when work improves the diet and health of children, it can help their schooling: intervention should focus on relieving poverty rather than preventing work.

On the other hand, most working children combine school and work, as did the Canadian children mentioned above. There is no evidence that limited and appropriate work detracts from school performance at any age. In some situations, the failure of the school system drives children to work: in rural Ethiopia, for example, children were observed to start skipping classes to go to work in the absence of teachers (Morrow, Tafere, and Vennam 2014): elite people have an image of well-resourced schools offering a wide variety of knowledge and experience; such schools are rarely available to poorer children. Some children and their families observe that school does not provide a reliable means to find jobs later in life and look to work experience as a backup and sometimes as a chance to learn a useful trade. These observations suggest that one way of reducing children's work would be to improve systems of schooling and ensure that they are well adapted to the social and economic environment in which the children live.

Children's education is more than schooling: home and the community also contribute, and work experience can be a constructive part of education understood broadly. Indeed, in the 1980s in Zimbabwe, there was a strong movement to combine education with productive work in a programme of "Education with Production", which was largely dropped from mainstream schooling in the face of a more rigid academic approach to education; the practical approach to education remained appreciated by some families (McLaughlin et al. 2002). More broadly, work experience, as in apprenticeships, can acquaint children with business skills and networks that are not provided in purely technical training programmes. At the level of the needs of individual children, some children have a poor aptitude for schoolwork and may find more rewarding occupations in work (Call and Mortimer 2001). In such cases, preventing children from working is not helpful: intervention should focus on improving schooling. It has been pointed out that children and their families could benefit from schools accommodating times when families need more hands-on their farms, such as at harvest time (Orkin 2012). If we want to protect children in relation to their education, we need to consider the needs and realistic possibilities for the specific children we wish to protect.

Local knowledge and children's voices

These considerations require knowledge of the local contexts, which takes time and effort to acquire. The people who have this knowledge are local communities, who are generally motivated to promote the well-being and development of their children. The Tonga study mentioned above illustrates how adults in local communities can take for granted the customary tasks of children without appreciating how they can interfere with the study that school encompasses; nevertheless, local communities are in a good position to identify children most in need of protection, and what is needed to improve their lives. An efficient way to find out which children need protection from harmful or exploitative work, and to find out what these children need to improve their lives and so to avoid harmful labour, is to work with local communities.

Even more important is to listen to those most affected by, and concerned with, the benefits and harms of working: the children themselves. The UN Convention on the Rights of the Child (UNCRC, article 12) and the African Charter on the Rights and Welfare of the Child (ACRWC, article 7) both assert the right of children to be heard in matters that affect their lives. Yet the voices of working children are consistently excluded from international conferences on child labour organised by the International Labour Organisation, which is the dominant force in international policies on child labour (Daalen 2023).

A contrasting approach is to focus on the perspectives of the children (see the essays in Hungerland et al. 2007). Working children frequently point out that they want to work to improve their own lives and to support their families: they feel proud to contribute to their families and want their work to be valued. They are aware that work sometimes interferes with schooling, and that it can be exploitative, but they have their ways of trying to reduce the risks arising in and from their work (Morrow and Vennam 2012). If we wish to safeguard them from such work, rather than remove their chosen opportunities, it would be more effective to support them in their own efforts to improve their lives and to protect their interests and rights.

In South America, Africa and Asia, working children have been supported in forming their organisations (Daalen 2020). In January 2023, Kigali (Rwanda) saw a 'Global Gathering of Working Children and Youth', with 63 child representatives from 16 countries, largely representatives of working children's organisations in Africa and Latin America. They formulated a declaration with five principal points needing the attention of society and governments:

- *Address poverty, provide decent jobs for our parents and ensure our basic needs are met.* Much of children's involvement in work is due to poverty: societies should ensure that their parents can earn adequate incomes.

- *Take our education seriously and provide quality education and skill training.* Quality education is not available to many children; it should include skills training appropriate to their environments.

- *Protect us from labour exploitation, harsh conditions and risks, and allow children to do suitable dignified work.* They point out that they do not want to stop all forms of work. In discussion, working children have pointed out that the failure of governments and trade unions to recognise their work means that they do not receive the legal protection from exploitation afforded to formally employed adults.

- *Listen to us, understand us and implement laws that respect our rights.*

- *Prevent and protect working children from violence and discrimination.* They point out that they "also experience violence and discrimination from police and other adults who are supposed to protect us".

The first point draws attention to a weakness of many protective programmes against the exploitation of children, which focus on employers and parents, and fail to take adequate account of violence against children at the societal level. Research has shown that large numbers of children suffer, and they suffer more, from societal problems like poverty: since poverty is both harmful to children and is strongly associated with other crimes of violence against children, policies that create poverty or fail to deal with it in effect constitute "structural violence", that is, a persistent societal form of abusive violence against children (Gil 1973: 14). This suggests that the most effective way of addressing the exploitative work of children is to address poverty in their communities, as working children themselves point out: indeed, social protection programmes have frequently proved successful in this regard (ILO 2017: 34–40; Streuli 2012).

The kind of protection the children's declaration calls for is complex. Organisations concerned with protecting children from exploitative and harmful work may well find it simpler to ban children from economic work. Moreover, some people argue that a total ban has the advantage of setting the same high standards for the childhoods of the poor as those enjoyed by more wealthy societies.

On the other hand, setting unrealistic standards does not attend to the structural violence behind children's abusive work. Nor does this simplified approach take into account the different needs of children in the face of the gross economic inequalities, both between nations and within nations, that are so evident in the contemporary world. If a grossly unequal society allows widespread poverty in its population, a few children may still be able to break out of poor communities through education and enterprise; but the majority will need to learn how to manage their lives in a community living in a state of high risk and few resources. Children need to acquire skills for life in such communities, skills that are not readily acquired in most formal schools. The lack of attention to these societal issues partly explains the long-standing failure of campaigns to eliminate child labour. Another serious weakness of classic elimination approaches is the damage they do to the limited opportunities available to children in deprived communities.

Thus, as well as protection from harmful labour, working children need protection from harmful interventions. In the field of children's work and labour, a narrow focus on the prevention of harm can damage the lives of the children most in need of protection. To avoid this kind of damage, we should focus on what children need to develop physically, socially, and cognitively in their specific social contexts. We should take account of the full range of effects arising from interventions, and verify that interventions do improve their lives. This involves paying attention to the whole context in which the children are conducting their lives, including their perceptions of the world they live in. Our interventions are more likely to be helpful if we first listen to children and find out what they consider important. I shall now suggest that parallel considerations could be helpful in other areas of child protection.

Protection against the Sexual Abuse of Children

The importance of touch

Child Psychologist Tiffany Field (2014) explored the developmental and therapeutic benefits to young children of touch. She opened her discussion with an account from the early 1990s of under-staffed orphanages in Romania where infants were largely left in cribs, and, deprived of the necessary consistent touch, they remained very undeveloped physically and in every other way. She commented, "Amazingly, at the same time that American television viewers were cringing at the sight of the Romanian orphans, American teachers were being instructed not to touch their students for fear of sexual abuse lawsuits" (Tiffany Field 2014). Although instances of child sexual abuse in schools were very rare, policies were being enforced that deprived children of beneficial touch within these institutions from infancy through to their teenage years. While this is a problem for North American society, negative perceptions of touch are appearing in child protection policies everywhere.

In many mammalian species, constant parental attentive touch is essential to the development of infants. The research of Field and others has established that touch can stimulate growth in infants; massage can be especially beneficial in infants born prematurely, and for other children who are in any way deprived of touch. On the other hand, inadequate physical human contact in infancy adversely affects their development, including the development of the brain and mind; such privation can be particularly damaging to children living in institutions.

The importance of early attachments to child development and subsequent behavioural patterns has long been well established (Bowlby 1969). Physical contact plays an important role in the development of attachments and the variations between different kinds of attachments. Touch continues to play a significant role in communication and relationships into adult life (Levy 2022; for a survey of recent research on the effects of affective interpersonal touch, see Crucianelli and Filippetti 2020). Although acceptable public display of interpersonal touch varies in different cultures, touch operates like facial expression and other forms of body language to convey emotions and intentions. Since sound supportive relationships are a key factor in long-term human well-being (Waldinger 2015), anything that contributes to the formation of such relationships must but an important component in children's development.

On the negative side, psychologist James Prescott showed that violent behaviour relates to touch deprivation: cross-culturally, he argued that where child-rearing practices encourage touch, societies tend to be less violent than those in which touch is discouraged (Prescott 1996). Field (2014, chapter 1) points to studies of differences between French and American societies: French parents played and spoke with their children and touched them more than did American parents, and the American children were more aggressive in their behaviour towards each other.

Research is ongoing into the physiological mechanisms behind the developmental effects of touch. Touch is associated with processes in the body that promote calm and relieve stress, making appropriate touch significant in healing and dealing with trauma (Eckstein et al. 2020). Apart from the affectionate touch from other humans, such beneficial effects can be acquired from touch by animals and even robots. This explains why concerned touch is instinctively a component of compassionate behaviour. Recent research indicates that compassion is important not only for the well-being of those in need of care but also for the well-being of those who exercise it. The Stanford School of Medicine, California, has established a centre for research on compassion, which argues that the practice of compassion is as important for health as physical exercise and a healthful diet (Stanford Medicine 2023). Since touch frequently provides the most effective way of exercising compassion, restrictions on compassionate touch are likely to impinge on the well-being of those in need of support, those wishing to offer support, and the social benefits of a compassionate society.

In mammalian species generally, the separation cries of infants and young who are unable (temporarily) to access comfort from their established carers is one of the most poignant expressions of distress: ethologist Frans de Waal argued that the evolution of compassion in mammals is rooted in response to such cries (Waal 1996). In many species, this response is confined to cries of children in one's genetic pool, but in humans, the instinct to respond to distressed cries of infants is much broader, often extending even to the young of other species. Separation, whether brief or extended, from the carers is a common cause of traumatic stress in children, and this is when they especially need comforting action. A culture that deprives caring touch to distressed young is abusive rather than protective.

With all these proven benefits conveyed by touch, why is there so much regulation against it? The problem is that some touch is harmful rather than beneficial. In certain situations, touch – or particular kinds of touch – can be unwelcome, disturbing, and even abusive. Besides being a component of affectionate and supporting behaviour, touch is also a component of aggressive and dominating behaviour, particularly sexual domination.

Welcome and unwelcome touch

A variety of factors can make touch welcome or unwelcome: where on the body and how the touch takes place, the relationships between the persons concerned, the respective genders of the parties, perceived motives for the touch, and cultural expectations all play a role in influencing whether or not a touch is welcome and consensual (Suvilheto et al. 2015). Even within cultures, there can be variations: what may be culturally acceptable behaviour among adult men in a particular society (for example, the freedom enjoyed by a mother's brother) may not be so acceptable to young girls who are subject to it. The boundaries are not always clear between beneficial and abusive touch. It is not, therefore, easy to regulate what touch is acceptable and what is not.

When I was younger, social workers were routinely taught to distinguish between "good touch" and "bad touch"; now they are commonly taught the simple rule – "no touch". The simple rule is useful for institutions and the adults working in them, who are often concerned about the possibility of lawsuits arising from accusations of abuse. Such lawsuits can adversely affect children served by these institutions. Nevertheless, restrictive rules against touch can deprive, for example, a traumatised child (or indeed a traumatised adult) of the best treatment to reduce stress. More generally, since touch is important in a variety of human relations, rules against touch can restrict the development of relationships that could contribute to the overall growth and well-being of children in a variety of situations. If young children, for their safety, are indoctrinated about the dangers of being touched, we are creating a society in which even those who care for us are treated with suspicion. Such attitudes hinder the development of a kind compassionate society that is beneficial to all.

If the best interests of children are to be our prime consideration (as demanded by UNCRC, article 3.1, ACRWC, article 4.1), the benefits of protection against abuse should be weighed against the harm of lost opportunities for the development of supportive relationships and social development. As Tiffany Field points out, instances of sexual abuse by teachers in schools in the USA are very rare, bringing into question rules that are costly to the development of confident relations between teachers and children generally. Here in Africa, we should be cautious about adopting such questionable standards.

The need to weigh costs against benefits is particularly important in residential institutions, where children are deprived by the nature of their situation of a more intimate home environment in which to grow in openly affectionate relationships. On the one hand, the need and craving for affection on the part of such children makes them particularly vulnerable to abuse. On the other hand, any further diminishing of the scarce tangible affection received by them can have damaging consequences. In the long term, abuse of such children can exacerbate the disadvantages of their situation; on the other hand, failure to acquire stable and affectionate relationships with adults in childhood and youth can make them particularly vulnerable later in life to any who appear to offer affection. Without the youthful experience of sound affectionate relationships, it is difficult for them later to discern and develop the kind of relationships that provide their best hope for good and constructive lives.

Institutions serving children are particularly vulnerable to accusations of abuse: an incident of abuse in an institution that is supposed to be caring for children makes a sensational news story. Apart from the scandal of harming children, such an incident can involve expensive litigation. And damage to the institution is likely to be damaging to the children in its care. It is understandable and right that institutions pay attention to visible policies and practices explicitly directed at keeping children in their charge safe from abuse. My point is that the emotional and developmental needs of the children are easily overlooked in safeguarding programmes when they should be a serious consideration in the formulation of these policies and practices.

The issue of touch has been used so far as a warning against simplistic policies on keeping children safe. Protection from harmful touch is necessary. However, a narrow focus on avoiding harmful touch can be damaging to children's physical and social development by severely limiting beneficial touch.

Broader safeguarding policies

Similar considerations apply to broader safeguarding policies. Keeping children safe through controls that limit their access to broader society can deprive them of a variety of opportunities to grow and develop. Such controls are most easily and urgently applied to the institutional care of vulnerable children; on the other hand, these are the children most in need of developing relationships with outsiders. It is important that safeguarding policies protect children's opportunities to develop constructive relationships and responsibility for themselves and their communities.

In practice, strict adherence to child safeguarding protocols can inhibit friendly and supportive relations; for example, when teachers are not allowed discretion on whether to report certain topics to authorities, children are reluctant – with good reason – to mention such topics in talking to a teacher. In practice, this removes a potential avenue of support for some children who are having problems at home. One problem in safeguarding children against sexual abuse is that adults widely find it difficult to speak to children about sexual topics. In the adult world, sex is necessary for the continuation of our families and humanity, and it is a source of conflict and confusion amid a wide range of standards of behaviour and interpersonal relations. We like romantically to think of children as innocent of these adult problems, almost as if they belong to a different species that is without sexual instincts and behaviour. Perhaps we forget our childhoods in which we explored with curiosity and learned from other children – not always accurately – on topics about which adults were reluctant to speak to us.

In the United Kingdom, concerns about protecting children from sexual abuse have resulted in restrictions in institutional settings such as schools that inhibit access of children to outsiders and even impede confident relations between teachers and children. The prescribed ideal of childhood purity seems poorly related to children's current world: a recent report (Wright 2023) on conversations over six years with 10,000 children and young people aged from 6 to around 22 years, of different backgrounds from around the nation, revealed that it is common for children aged six to encounter pornography on line; for nine- to eleven-year-olds, exposure is frequent. These revelations were often new to the parents. While we might dismiss this as a problem of a wealthy society with widespread access to smartphones and the internet, we can learn from their mistakes to ensure that here in Africa our safeguarding practices take fully into account the social context in which our children live. Especially in under-resourced and crowded living conditions, the sexual behaviour of adults is not hidden from children.

Way Forward

This chapter has so far pointed out that attempts to keep children safe from exploitative labour can have the unintended consequence of depriving children of opportunities to grow in the lives of the communities in which they live and of opportunities to improve their lives. Similarly, attempts to avoid risks of child sexual abuse can restrict children's personal and social development. Nevertheless, the need to protect children from exploitation and all kinds of abuse remains an important right for children and a responsibility for adults. Such tension between the need for protection on the one hand, and possible negative consequences of protective policies on the other, spreads generally to interventions in the field of child protection.

There have been cases where well-intentioned interventions in support of children had unintended consequences that deprived some children of intended benefits and sometimes damaged their life chances (Bourdillon and Myers 2013). The cases came from Africa, Asia, the Middle East, and Latin America. They ranged in content, including children caught up in conflict or trying to escape from it; work, migration and trafficking; help for orphans who missed the greater need to deal with societal poverty; harmful traditional practices; replacing corporal punishment with alternatives that proved to be socially disruptive; and the bureaucratic practice of social welfare. Arising from these studies (Myers and Bourdillon 2012) are five general lessons for consideration in future practice, which apply to our situations in Zimbabwe and in Africa more generally.

First, the protection of children involves much more than keeping them safe; the objective of protective programmes must ultimately be children's well-being and development. A narrow focus on avoiding harm can raise serious problems for children. There is a danger that making child protection a field for specialist individuals and organisations could encourage such a narrow focus; perhaps protection could be better understood as a component of educational and developmental programmes.

Further, children's individual development takes place in a social context and leads to life in a particular society. To be useful to children in the long term, the acquisition of social and life skills needs to be appropriate to the settings in which the children are likely to conduct their lives. This observation leads to a second lesson: the protection of children's well-being and development must fit their social and economic context and requires the involvement of their communities and families. Such involvement is a useful check against the arbitrary imposition of outside or dominant cultures. More fundamentally, without the cooperation of local communities, to rely on the law and its enforcement is likely to fail children. When the local environment is hostile to laws imposed from above, the result can be serious problems for children.

A corollary to considering the social environment is that the protection of children should not ignore structural violence against children. We cannot protect children from harmful work while the greater violence of poverty and hunger drives them into it. It is difficult to protect children from sexual abuse while allowing pornographic videos to pop up on their phones. More generally, we cannot claim to be protecting children while we contribute to the destruction of the environment on which we all have to depend.

A third lesson relates to a fundamental human right of children (UNCRC, article 3; ACRWC, article 4): in interventions for children, children's interest must be the primary consideration. The interests of institutions and supporting adults are important: they need finance and societal approval to serve children. But these interests should be explicitly subsidiary to the interests of the children they are serving.

The fourth lesson is related to this: all policies, programmes, and activities for children should be judged according to their outcomes in terms of the well-being and development of the affected children. Interventions are for children only if children are better off as a result. These outcomes must go beyond the immediate safety of children: they should include their prospective ability as adults to live independently, to fit constructively into society, and to establish relationships that are supportive of individuals and communities.

Perhaps the most important lesson is that to ensure protective policies and programmes are beneficial to children, it is necessary to consult with children and to take their opinions seriously. The right of children to have a say in matters that affect their lives according to their level of maturity and competence, and to have their opinions taken seriously, is widely acknowledged. Nevertheless, in matters of child protection adults in Africa as elsewhere habitually assume that they know what is best for the children, and that the protection of children is their responsibility. When young people make demands that fall outside the boundaries of what adults perceive to be protective, their views are readily dismissed based on immaturity: our instinct to protect children often overrides the children's right to self-determination (Peleg 2018).

Conclusion

To conclude, the responsibility to guide and protect children must include keeping open opportunities for them to grow and develop their own lives. If society fails to keep such opportunities open, it will not be giving them the protection they need. Indeed, children, especially young children, are not always aware of the risks and hazards in their environment, and they do not always give adequate attention to long-term development. Adults rightly take on the responsibility of guiding and teaching young people. Children may have to be pressurised, for example, to undertake schoolwork for their long-term benefit, or to behave in ways acceptable to the society on which they depend as social beings. On the other hand, adults do not always get things right, and children – even young children – may see dangers and problems that are missed by adults. For example, consultation with children in Thailand proved helpful in identifying areas of danger and formulating a protective programme relating to information technology (Cook et al. 2012). The ability of organisations of working children to support each other and to develop strategies for the protection and support of working children. Magdalene Muoki (2015) describes how working children were able to influence policy and decisions concerning their work in Kenya.

It helps to respect children as human beings, like ourselves. While they generally have less knowledge and experience than adults, they nevertheless do learn from very real and varied experiences. Among other things, the development of information technology and the rapidly deteriorating climate make their social environment very different from that in which we grew up. They develop their dreams and expectations, not always realistic, but important to the way their lives are developing. They have their agency as they try to direct the course of their own lives. The society and environment they will be living in as adults will be different from what we have now. Since society does not have solutions to many problems they will face, they must be enabled to develop their solutions.

References

BBC, 2023. "The Night They Came for Our Children." *BBC Africa Eye* documentary. Accessed October 26, 2023. https://www.youtube.com/watch?v=TKHKjZ77RC0.

BOURDILLON Michael. 1994. "Street Children in Harare." *Africa* 64 (4): 134–152.

___, 1999. *Earn-and-Learn: Work for Education in the Eastern Highlands of Zimbabwe.* Accessed October 26, 2023. https://www.academia.edu/6328045/Earn-and-learn_Work_for_Education_in_the_Eastern_Highlands_of_Zimbabwe.

___, ed. 2000. *Earning a Life: Working Children in Zimbabwe.* Harare: Weaver Press.

___, 2009. "A Place for Work in Children's Lives?" Plan Canada, Save the Children Canada. Accessed March 11, 2013. https://resource centre.savethechildren.net/node/4087/pdf/4087.pdf.

___, 2016. "Earn-and-Learn: Schools on Tea Estates in Zimbabwe." Children&Work Case Studies. *Children&Work Network.* Accessed October 26, 2023. https://www.childrenandwork.net/earn-and-learn.

___, 2017. "Labor as Education." In *Laboring and Learning*, edited by Tatek Abebe and Johanna Waters. *Geographies of Children and Young People.* New York: Springer.

BOURDILLON Michael, LEVISON Deborah, MYERS William and WHITE Ben, 2010. *Rights and Wrongs of Children's Work.* Edited by Myra Bluebond-Langner. *Rutgers Series in Childhood Studies.* New Brunswick, NJ: Rutgers University Press.

BOURDILLON Michael, and MUSVOSVI Eve. 2014. "What Can Children's Rights Mean When Children Are Struggling to Survive? The Case of Chiweshe, Zimbabwe." In *Children's Lives in an Era of Children's Rights: The Progress of the Convention on the Rights of the Child in Africa*, edited by Nicola Ansell and Afua Twum-Danso Imoh, 105–122. London: Routledge.

BOURDILLON Michael and MYERS William, eds. 2013. *Child Protection in Development.* Abingdon: Routledge.

BOWLBY John, 1969. *Attachment.* New York: Basic Books.

CALL Kathleen T. and MORTIMER Jeylan T., 2001. *Arenas of Comfort in Adolescence: A Study of Adjustment in Context.* Mahwah, NJ, and London: Lawrence Erlbaum Associates.

COOK Philip H., HEYKOOP Cheryl, ANUNTAVORASKUL Athapol and VIBULPHOL Jutarat, 2012. "Action Research Exploring Information Communication Technologies (ICT) and Child Protection in Thailand." *Development in Practice* 22 (4): 574–587.

CRUCIANELLI Laura and FILIPPETTI Marta L., 2020. "Developmental Perspectives on Interpersonal Affective Touch." *Topoi* 39: 575–586. https://doi.org/10.1007/s11245-018-9565-1.

DE WAAL Frans, 1996. *Good Natured: The Origins of Right and Wrong in Humans and Other Animals.* Cambridge, MA, and London: Harvard University Press.

ECKSTEIN Monika, MAMAEV Ilshat, DITZEN Beate and SAILER Uta, 2020. "Calming Effects of Touch in Human, Animal, and Robotic Interaction— Scientific State-of-the-Art and Technical Advances." *Frontiers in Psychiatry* 11. https://doi.org/10.3389/fpsyt.2020.555058.

FIELD Tiffany. 2014. *Touch.* Cambridge, MA: MIT Press.

FRANCAVILLA Chiara, AFREH-NUAMAH Kwakye and BOATENG Kyenkyenhene, 2023. "Ghanaian Children Taken from Home Over False Trafficking Claims." *BBC News.* Accessed October 26, 2023. https://www.bbc.co.uk/news/world-africa-66122058.

GIL David G., 1973. *Violence Against Children.* Cambridge, MA: Harvard University Press.

HUNGERLAND Beatrice, LIEBEL Manfred, MILNE Brian and WIHSTUTZ Anne, eds. 2007. *Working to Be Someone: Child Focused Research and Practice with Working Children.* London and Philadelphia: Jessica Kingsley.

ILO, 2017. *Ending Child Labour by 2025: A Review of Policies and Programmes.* Geneva: International Labour Organization.

KAHNEMAN Daniel, 2011. *Thinking, Fast and Slow.* New York: Farrar, Straus, and Giroux.

LEVY Terry M., 2022. "Why Is Touch So Important for Attachment?" Evergreen Psychotherapy Center. Last Modified April 20, 2022. Accessed October 26, 2023. https://evergreenpsychotherapycenter.com/why-is-touch-so-important-for-attachment/.

MAPEDZAHAMA Virginia and BOURDILLON Michael, 2000. "Working Street Children in Harare." In *Earning a Life*, edited by Michael Bourdillon, 25–44. Harare: Weaver Press.

MCLAUGHLIN Janice, NHUNDU Vimbisai, MLAMBO Phares and CHUNG Fay, 2002. *Education with Production in Zimbabwe: The Story of ZIMFEP.* Harare: Zimbabwe Foundation for Education with Production (ZIMFEP) & Foundation for Education with Production (FEP).

MORROW Virginia, TAFERE Yisak and VENNAM Uma, 2014. "Changes in Rural Children's Use of Time: Evidence from Ethiopia and Andhra Pradesh, India." In *Growing Up in Poverty*, edited by Michael Bourdillon and Jo Boyden, 139–160. *Palgrave Studies on Children and Development.* Basingstoke: Palgrave Macmillan.

MORROW Virginia and VENNAM Uma, 2012. "Children's Responses to Risk in Agricultural Work in Andhra Pradesh, India." *Development in Practice* 22 (4): 549–561.

MUOKI Magdalene Wanza, 2015. "The Role of Child Participation in Influencing Policies to Protect Children from Harmful Work: A Kenyan Case." In *Children's Work and Labour in East Africa: Social Context and Implications for Policy*, edited by Alula Pankhurst, Michael Bourdillon, and Gina Crivello, 163–170. Addis Ababa: OSSREA.

MURRAY Helen, 2014. "Fulfilling the Promise of School Education? Factors Shaping Education Inequalities in Ethiopia, India, Peru and Vietnam." In *Growing Up in Poverty*, edited by Michael Bourdillon and Jo Boyden. Basingstoke: Palgrave Macmillan.

MYERS William, and BOURDILLON Michael, 2012. "Concluding Reflections: How Might We Really Protect Children?" *Development in Practice* 22 (4): 613–620.

OKYERE Samuel, 2014. "Children's Participation in Prohibited Work in Ghana and Its Implication for the Convention on the Rights of the Child." In *Children's Lives in an Era of Children's Rights: The Progress of the Convention on the Rights of the Child in Africa*, edited by Nicola Ansell and Afua Twum-Danso Imoh, 92–104. London: Routledge.

ORKIN Kate, 2012. "Are Work and Schooling Complementary or Competitive for Children in Rural Ethiopia? A Mixed-Methods Study." In *Childhood Poverty: Multidisciplinary Approaches*, edited by Jo Boyden and Michael Bourdillon, 298–313. Basingstoke: Palgrave Macmillan.

PELEG Noam, 2018. "Illusion of Inclusion: Challenging Universalist Conceptions in International Children's Rights Law." *Australian Journal of Human Rights* 24 (3): 326–344. https://doi.org/10.1080/1323238X.2018.1542924.

PRESCOTT James W., 1996. "The Origins of Human Love and Violence." *Pre-and Perinatal Psychology Journal* 10 (3): 143–188.

RABY Rebecca and SHEPPARD Lindsay C., 2023. "'It's Intimidating Going into Your First Job': Young Teens and Workplace Safety." *Youth Studies* 27 September 2023.

REYNOLDS Pamela, 1991. *Dance Civet Cat: Child Labour in the Zambezi Valley.* Harare: Baobab Books.

SHUMBA Ngoni, 2015. "Zimbabwe: When Ending Child Labour Does Not End Child Exploitation." *African Arguments.* Accessed November 20, 2015. https://africanarguments.org/2015/09/10/zimbabwe-when-ending-child-labour-does-not-end-child-exploitation/.

STANFORD MEDICINE, 2023. "The Center for Compassion and Altruism Research and Education: Mission & Vision." Accessed November 7, 2023. https://ccare.stanford.edu/about/mission-vision/.

STREULI Natalia, 2012. "Child Protection: A Role for Conditional Cash Transfer Programmes?" *Development in Practice* 22 (4): 588–599.

SUVILHETO Juulia T., GLEREAN Enrico, DUNBAR Robin I. M., HARI Riita and NUMMENMAA Laura, 2015. "Topography of Social Touching Depends on Emotional Bonds Between Humans." *PNAS* 112 (45): 13811–13816. https://doi.org/10.1073/pnas.1519231112.

VAN DAALEN Edward, 2020. "Working Children's Movements." In *The SAGE Encyclopedia on Children and Childhood Studies*, edited by Daniel Thomas Cook, 1676–1679. Thousand Oaks: Sage.

___, 2023. "'Could It Be That They Do Not Want to Hear What We Have to Say?' Organised Working Children and the International Politics and Representations of Child Labour." In *The Politics of Children's Rights and Representation*, edited by Bengt Sandin, Jonathan Josefsson, Karl Hanson, and Sarada Balagopalan, 131–160. *Studies in Childhood and Youth.* Cham, Switzerland: Palgrave Macmillan.

WALDINGER Robert, 2015. "What Makes a Good Life? Lessons from the Longest Study on Happiness." *TEDx.* Accessed November 4, 2023. https://www.ted.com/talks/robert_waldinger_what_makes_a_good_life_lessons_from_th e_longest_study_on_happiness.

WOUANGO Josephine, 2015. "Children's Perspectives on Their Working Lives and on Public Action Against Child Labour in Burkina Faso." In *Children's Work and Labour in East Africa: Social Context and Implications for Policy*, edited by Alula Pankhurst, Michael Bourdillon, and Gina Crivello, 125–142. Addis Ababa: OSSREA.

WRIGHT Abbey, 2023. "Too Much Too Young: I Talked to 10,000 Children About Pornography. Here Are 10 Things I Learned." *The Guardian*, September 13, 2023. https://www.theguardian.com/society/2023/sep/13/adults-are-terrified-of -talking-to-us-about-it-10-things-i-learned-from-children-about-pornography/.

Implementation of the Legislations for Child Protection in Africa, Checks and Balances: A Systematic Review

Francis Maushe, Ruth Muregi,
Vongai P Mangwiro, Witness Chikoko

Introduction

The abuse of children and the lack of their protection in some parts of Africa has become a central issue in debates. For the past three decades, African countries have adopted and signed several legislative frameworks meant to safeguard children from various forms of abuse. The world is struggling with the rising cases of various forms of child abuse. These various forms of child abuse especially physical and sexual abuse have become a serious problem that the world is grappling with. Bodkin, Pivnick, Bondy, Ziegler and Jernigan (2019) traced the history of childhood abuse and its effects on adulthood. A literature search of unique studies from 1429 records revealed that half of the people in Canadian prisons experienced abuse in their childhood. This implies the negative implications of childhood abuse on the adulthood of an individual. Child abuse cases increased during COVID-19, where the perpetrators' presence in the home due to restrictions exposed children to abuse.

Child abuse is reported to be occurring in various ways across the world. Calls for child protection are primarily influenced by the continuation of children's exposure to unscrupulous and devastating consequences that militate against their developmental milestones (Bodkin et al. 2019). The world, especially developing countries, is losing momentum towards maximized economic performance due to the existence of child abuse cases where some children drop out of school, experience mental health problems, are exposed to chronic health conditions, and even die due to abuse. An effort to unravel the prevalence of child abuse cases in the world particularly in Africa shapes directions for the betterment of the future of children and the strengthening of child protection measures. Child protection measures are connected to the Sustainable Development Goals

Agenda (SDGs) where member countries should ensure they maximize the protection of children in all walks of life.

Child Abuse in Africa

Child abuse in Africa is still a problem, with members having historically been faced with and are yet to find lasting solutions. Many African countries have ratified and signed several laws, policies, and programmes to promote the protection of children, especially the girl child. The African Partnership to End Violence Against Children (APEVAC, 2021) raised concerns about the prevalence of child abuse in Africa with high rates of physical, sexual, and psychological violence alleged to be increasingly growing based on several factors. Most worryingly is the reason behind the increase in child abuse cases despite the existence of several legislative frameworks meant to curb child abuse APEVAC (2021) revealed that more than half a million children in Africa experience various forms of abuse among which sexual abuse is most reported. Katz, Carmit, Sabine, Annie, et al. (2021) state that the increase in child abuse cases was witnessed in South Africa during the COVID-19 era in which child protection services were less effective given the limitations that were caused by COVID-19. School closures and the lockdown restrictions created more limitations to the monitoring of child abuse cases.

Nigeria is one of the countries which experiences high rates of child abuse given the Boko haram attacks in the nation. The last decade in Africa has been faced with gross violations of human rights especially children, with major legislative frameworks such as the United Nations Convention on the Rights of the Child that was signed and ratified having not brought significant interventions for Nigeria. For example, Nigeria became the second highest country with children who were recruited by armed groups and the 3rd in terms of abductions that also involved children. Disconcerting is the fact that these human rights violations on children are happening in the presence of various laws that protect children as well as government departments and stakeholders who are responsible for enforcing the implementation of these laws.

Child Abuse in Zimbabwe

Child abuse cases in Zimbabwe have also been more pronounced based on media reports and organizations which focus on children's welfare. Several cases of child abuse have been masked in Zimbabwe, with children, particularly the girl child, more exposed to the dangers of the world. Childline (2022) reveals that children are abused by their relatives, neighbours, own parents, and even their siblings and the various forms of abuse negatively impact children's developmental milestones. Zimbabwe is a signatory to several global, regional, and national child protection laws and its departments such as the Home Affairs, Department of Social Development (DSD), and Ministry of Health and Child Care among other concerned stakeholders, are implementing various programmes to ensure that children's rights are safeguarded. The Children's Act Chapter (5:06) promotes the protection of children from abuse informed by the country's national constitution. Moyo (2021) outlined the overarching accounts of child abuse cases in which the Zimbabwe National Statistics Agency (ZIMSTATS) reported the murders of 22 children during the period 2019-2020 at the hands of parents and guardians, which is a red flag regarding child protection efforts in Zimbabwe.

It is disheartening to have increased reports of child abuse cases in Zimbabwe despite the country being a signatory of powerful legal instruments such as the United Nations Convention on the Rights of the Child (UNCRC) and the African Charter on the Rights and Welfare of the Child (ACRWC). Shilpa, Shanmugam, Obongo, Mupambireyi, Kasese, Bangani, & Miller (2021) obtained in their study that the existing harsh economic conditions are making child protection efforts difficult. On the other hand, Shilpa et al. (2021) argue that poor home environments and inept leadership in the implementation of child protection services are some of the factors triggering the increase in child abuse in the country. Coupled with people's high involvement in drug and substance abuse, children are on the verge of being physically, emotionally, and sexually abused at the expense of their future cognitive development adventures. The Zimbabwe National Council for the Welfare of Children (ZNCWC) also argues that COVID-19 worsened children's situation in terms of their exposure to abuse particularly in homes and this drove some of them into the streets. There is limited literature pointing to the effectiveness of legislative frameworks in protecting children from abuse in Africa. It is within this pretext that this systematic literature review focused on literature within the African context that focuses on the implementation of child protection laws and assessing the successes and failures in that regard.

Based on this background, child abuse is highly prevalent across the world but Zimbabwe seems to also have higher margins of child abuse cases, which poses a question if the existing legal frameworks are being effectively implemented as well as if they are functional. For example, Childline Zimbabwe (2021) states that they received 25 000 cases during the period of 2020 of child abuse of which 26% accounted for sexual abuse in which the girl child was the most affected. Huge gaps are evident in the Zimbabwe perspective regarding efforts to combat child abuse through legislation, given the continued reports of child abuse cases and the proliferation of new forms of child abuse such as child trafficking, high suicidal rates among children, and an increase in child marriages and child prostitution.

It is important to assess the implementation of legislation for child protection in Africa (successes and failures) and establish the best interventions to enhance child protection in Africa. The major objectives of the systematic review were; to assess the existing legislation being implemented in Africa to protect children, to explore the challenges being faced in implementing child protection laws, and to establish interventions that can be used to enhance the enforcement of legislation to maximize the achievement of child protection goals.

Legislations for Child Protection in Africa

Child protection in Africa is informed by several legal instruments while each country has its laws and policies that are grounded on regional and global laws on child protection. The majority of the 58 countries in Africa ratified and signed laws for protecting children to eradicate cases of child abuse, mainly sexual abuse and child marriages, physical abuse, and child trafficking among other forms of abuse. The major laws for child protection in Africa are shown in the table below.

Legal instrument (Year)	Description of major provisions
African Charter on the Rights and Welfare of the Child (1990) [ACRWC]	The treaty came into force in 1990 and was fully adopted in 1990. It sets out the rights and defines the principles for the status of children. Protects children from all forms of torture and inhuman or degrading treatment. For example, the Right to freedom from discrimination (Article 2), equality (Article 3), life and personal integrity (Article 4)
United Nations Convention on the Rights of the Child (UNCRC) (1989)	Describes the universal rights endowed to a child

Optional Protocols to the CRC	They include: i. Optional Protocol on the sale of children, child prostitution, and child pornography ii. Optional protocol on the Involvement of children in armed conflict iii. Optional Protocol on a communications procedure
ILO Convention on the Worst Forms of Child Labour (1999; 182)	Taking immediate action to prohibit and eliminate the worst forms of child labour (slavery, prostitution, and dangerous labour).

Table 2: Child protection legal instruments in Africa

The range of laws that promote child protection in Africa is fundamental to the eradication of child abuse and the improvement of economic development. However, Moyo (2021) argues that the existence of these strong legal instruments, conventions, and treaties did not achieve a milestone towards the expected child protection outcomes in the African continent. The continued rise in reports about sexual abuse is a true reflection of the hurdles of child protection efforts by African governments. Reviewing the literature in this chapter promoted the understanding of the best interventions to strengthen the effective implementation of various legal instruments for child protection in Africa. Additionally, the majority of African countries have national policies that promote child protection as well as Acts that guide child protection activities. In the same vein, African countries' constitutions also have provisions for the protection of children.

Implementation of Legislative Frameworks for Child Protection in Africa

In the same vein, the challenges that are experienced and the interventions to strengthen child protection mechanisms in Africa are analyzed in this section. Literature searches focused on literature published in the past 5 years on Google Scholar, PubMed, Scopas, and other manual searches of peer-reviewed articles. Direct quotations were used as supportive evidence in some parts of the data collection.

Legislation being implemented in Africa to protect children

There are various studies that have focused on legislation that is meant for child protection in the African context. Successes and failures of various African countries can be identified in literature regarding their progress in protecting children.

African Charter on the Rights and Welfare of the Child (1990)

The African Charter was found to be one of the most common laws for protecting children that is being implemented in African nations. Studies by Mezmur (2020) who explored the success of the Charter's implementation after 30 years found ground-breaking results, with the instrument having enabled the reduction of child abuse cases. However, despite the existence of the African Charter, countries such as Somalia, as reported in the media, have developed a draft Sexual Offences Bill that allows child marriages. This implies that the implementation of the regional laws is still far below the expected standards. In the same vein, Nigeria has been condemned by organizations such as UNICEF for its failure to adhere to the guidelines of the African Charter by sentencing a thirteen-year-old to 10 years. The majority of articles that were reviewed agreed that progress on the African Charter is slow given the rise of actions against its provisions in member states who ratified the same legal instrument (Dejo 2002, Chirwa 2002, Julia 2017, Elvis, Murungu, & Aman 2022, Mezmur 2020). The implementation of the African Charter based on the reviewed articles shows little progress commensurate with the SDGs as well as the reports about the rising cases of abuse. Several calls and complaints are being raised for SADC to take action to combat the proliferation of child mongers and other institutions and practices that exacerbate children's exposure to abuse.

Additionally, the review of the articles shows that the African Charter has transformed the child protection narrative in Africa by giving distinct guidelines on the management of childcare institutions and institutions that deal with children. According to Judith-Anne (2012), the African Charter on the Rights of the Child necessitated the fight against child marriages in which some of the perpetrators are brought to book. In the same vein, Tieku (2019) in his assessment of the successes and failures of the African Charter concluded that the Charter gave African nations one voice to speak against child abuse among other inhuman treatment against children. The articles agree on the successes of the African Charter in transforming some adverse cultural practices that promoted child marriages and other forms of child abuse.

International Instruments

Sam et al (2019), Fimin (2020), and Okyere (2019) established similar findings based on the success of the UNCRC on child protection in which children have been accorded an opportunity to get improved access to health, education, and being safeguarded from various forms of abuse. Petrowski et al. (2021) argued that despite the success of child protection legislation in Africa, violence against children still exists and it increased particularly during the Covid-19 era. Petrowski et al. (2021) concluded that child protection legislation empowered childcare institutions, governments, and helplines to protect children during the Covid-19 era although the restrictions limited the effectiveness of interventions to protect and safeguard children as well as helping the victims of abuse. Olayiwola (2021) and Isioma (2019) unravelled the high levels of child abuse in the form of abductions, and witchcraft stigmatization among other forms despite Nigeria being a signatory of the major Africa's child protection laws. The Boko Haram attacks in Nigeria that have affected the nation for the past 5 years are evidence of the country's failure to implement interventions to protect and safeguard children from being abused. Thousands of children were victimized resulting in deaths, child marriages, unwanted pregnancies, and diseases among others. This reflects loopholes aligned to the child protection laws that are not liberating children from torture among other forms of abuse in their respective countries.

Challenges being faced in implementing child protection laws in Africa

There are several challenges that African countries are experiencing in implementing child protection laws in promoting the eradication of child abuse. The literature reviewed unravelled the impact of the challenges that militate against child protection measures to ensure the welfare of children and the successes of government entities and other related professions such as Social Work. Most articles that were reviewed including Hafejee et al. (2020), Katz et al. (2022), Fermin (2020), and Nhapi (2020) highlighted in their findings that lack of resources is the major challenge that inhibits the effective implementation of child protection laws in African countries. Most African countries are still developing and are experiencing economic challenges that reduce their capacity to effectively strengthen the enforcement of local and regional child protection laws. For example, the recent massive exodus of Social

Workers from Zimbabwe for greener pastures in countries such as the UK, Canada, and Poland among others is a true reflection of the major impediment that is drawing back the success of legal child protection instruments for Africa since their establishment since this reflects enormous brain drain of technocrats responsible for the implementation of child protection laws.

Zimbabwe has long been held to account for human rights violations in which children are not excluded. Ringson and Chereni (2020) focused on the abuse and exploitation of OVCs by human rights organizations implying the continued existence of the plight of children despite the gaps within the implementation of these legal instruments. Additionally, Bengesai, Lateef, and Makonye (2021) revealed how the scourge of child marriages and rape still haunts the African continent. There is a strong connection between poverty and child marriages, such that the implementation of child protection laws cannot be effective if the communities are poor, and young girls will always be subjected to early marriages.

Lack of cohesiveness and poor government support was also highlighted in the articles that were reviewed. Adugna et al. (2020) and Russel et al. (2020) produced similar findings on the barriers to policy implementation for child protection in developing countries, where sexual abuse remains high because of poor policy implementation and uneven support provision by relevant ministries and stakeholders. In the same vein, it was revealed that without financial support, the implementation of child protection programmes will remain a mystery given several activities that should be carried out. Further, based on Sserwanja et al. (2021) article on increased child abuse in Uganda, lack of planning in government departments among other child welfare organizations remains an obstacle to the successful implementation of child protection laws for the betterment of the future of children and the functioning of African economies. Given the availability of adequate resources, and technical and financial support in African nations, the implementation of child protection legislation could have been a success now. Some countries such as Rwanda have managed to implement successful government programmes that have improved the welfare of children in terms of health, reducing mortality rates, increasing access to education, and reducing abuse cases (Benimana, 2022). Benimana's (2022) article showed that social workers' perspectives on child protection in Rwanda are similar to the South African context where some key indicators in child protection have been achieved. In reviewing the article by Haffejee et al. (2020), it was established that fruitful lessons were learned from

COVID-19 regarding the strengthening of child protection efforts in the South African context.

Interventions to Strengthen Legislation for Child Protection Goals

The systematic review of the literature also shows that those studies that managed to establish interventions have been successful in enhancing the implementation of child protection laws in Africa. The review made use of case studies of those articles that gave recommendations for effective child protection efforts. It was established from the majority of articles that were reviewed that increasing budget prioritization for child protection can strengthen the implementation of child protection laws. Hickey et al. (2023), Fokala et al. (2022), Isioma (2019), Benimana (2022), and Chirwa (2002) similarly pointed out the importance of funding programmes and activities aligned with the strengthening of child protection laws implementation. This has been evident in Africa's initiatives to promote the attainment of the UN SDGs on child protection by increasing the budgets of social welfare departments. The goals of child protection can be maximized through the availability of adequate financial resources that enable the training of various stakeholders to enhance child protection.

Decolonizing Children's Rights in Africa

There is need to decolonise children's rights in Africa as this will be a way of renewing and revisiting children's rights. To achieve decolonization of children's rights in Africa, a myriad of issues need to be attended to. These include issues to do with social justice to try and overthrow oppressive systems that suppress children's rights issues to do with inclusivity and diversity, and ensuring cultural sensitive laws and interventions. The colonial legacy has undeniably left a significant print on children's rights in Africa whereby the colonial giants set the standard aligning to their own beliefs and cultures without considering the African way of life.

In as much a complex move it could be to achieve total decolonization of children's rights in Africa, the cooperation of governments, regional and international organizations, and all stakeholders is undoubtedly an effective way to achieve such. The IKS is also not to be undermined as it offers practical channels of communication that will aid in upholding children's rights in a non-offensive way, thus preserving the African legacy. Intergenerational dialogues will facilitate the passage of important information that will support decolonization efforts whilst acknowledging and integrating indigenous knowledge into policies.

Recommendations

The chapter recommended the following:

- The SADC should set aside a fund that is sponsored by its member states to ensure the strengthening of mechanisms to monitor and supervise the implementation of child protection laws across Africa.

- African governments should intensify partnerships with organizations such as UNICEF among others to ensure they get adequate support in terms of training of various institutions to ensure the mainstreaming of child protection at various levels.

- SADC should emphasize good governance to its member states since good governance is the backbone of effective leadership that enables effective implementation of child protection laws.

- SADC countries should engage and share their successes and challenges in child protection and utilize that forum as a learning curve towards intensifying the implementation of child protection laws. This will promote the eradication of child abuse cases such as child marriages, rape, physical abuse, and sexual abuse among others.

- Countries in the African region should strengthen their cultural systems in which professions such as social work, education, and health should be adequately trained and resourced to enforce cultural principles of doing good to others. This will in turn eliminate harmful practices that perpetuate the abuse of children.

Conclusion

The chapter demonstrated that the implementation of child protection legislation in Africa has made significant progress, yet the ongoing occurrence of child abuse highlights critical gaps that need to be addressed. Despite the existence of comprehensive legal frameworks, such as the African Charter on the Rights and Welfare of the Child, the slow pace of enforcement raises concerns about their effectiveness in safeguarding children's rights and well-being. The chapter has also systematically reviewed the challenges hindering the successful implementation of these laws, including inadequate resources and a lack of strategic planning. To advance child protection in Africa, it is essential to prioritize budget allocations and promote public awareness initiatives that empower communities and encourage child participation in decision-making. Ultimately, addressing the gaps in legislation and implementation will be vital for achieving sustainable development goals and ensuring a safer environment for children in Africa.

References

AFROOZ KAVIANI Johnson and SLOTH-NIELSEN Julia, 2020. "Child Protection, Safeguarding and the Role of the African Charter on the Rights and Welfare of the Child: Looking Back and Looking Ahead." *African Human Rights Law Journal* 20 (2).

BENGESAI Annah V., AMUSA Lateef B. and MAKONYE Felix, 2021. "The Impact of Girl Child Marriage on the Completion of the First Cycle of Secondary Education in Zimbabwe: A Propensity Score Analysis." *PloS One* 16 (6): e0252413.

BENIMANA Geraldine, 2022. "Protection of Children Rights in Rwanda: Perspectives of Social Workers." PhD diss., Mykolo Romerio universitetas.

BENYAM Dawit Mezmur, 2020. "The African Children's Charter @30: A Distinction without a Difference?" *The International Journal of Children's Rights*.

BODKIN Claire, PIVNICK Lucie, BONDY Susan J., ZIEGLER Carolyn, MARTIN Ruth Elwood, JERNIGAN Carey and KOUYOUMDJIAN Fiona. 2019. "History of Childhood Abuse in Populations Incarcerated in Canada: A Systematic Review and Meta-Analysis." *American Journal of Public Health* 109 (3): e1–e11.

CHILD RIGHTS COALITION ASIA, 2016. "Violence Against Children Southeast Asia." Retrieved from: CRC_VACSASIA_FINAL.pdf (crcasia.org).

CHIRWA Danwood Mzikenge, 2002. "The Merits and Demerits of the African Charter on the Rights and Welfare of the Child." *International Journal of Children's Rights* 10: 157.

END VIOLENCE AGAINST CHILDREN, 2021. "New Data Shows Violence Against Children Is Rising across the African Continent."

FIRMIN Carlene, 2020. *Contextual Safeguarding and Child Protection: Rewriting the Rules.* Taylor & Francis.

FOKALA Elvis, MURUNGI Nkatha and AMAN Mai, eds. 2022. *The Status of the Implementation of the African Children's Charter: A Ten-Country Study.* Pretoria: University Law Press.

HAFFEJEE Sadiyya and THEMBEKILE LEVINE Diane, 2020. "'When Will I Be Free': Lessons from COVID-19 for Child Protection in South Africa." *Child Abuse & Neglect* 110: 104715.

HICKEY Sam, LAVERS Tom, NIÑO-ZARAZÚA Miguel and SEEKINGS Jeremy, 2019. *The Politics of Social Protection in Eastern and Southern Africa.* Oxford University Press.

INTEREST WATCH FOUNDATION, 2023. "EU Still Hosts the Most Child Sexual Abuse Material in the World." https://www.iwf.org.uk/news-media/news/eu-still-hosts-the-most-child-sexual-abuse-material-in-the-world/

ISIOMA Chineyemba Lydia, 2019. "Witchcraft Stigmatization and Abuse of Children in Akwa-Ibom State, Nigeria." *International Journal of Sociology and Anthropology* 11 (4): 43–53.

KATZ Ilan et al., 2021. "Child Maltreatment Reports and Child Protection Service Responses during COVID-19: Knowledge Exchange among Australia, Brazil, Canada, Colombia, Germany, Israel, and South Africa." *Child Abuse & Neglect* 116: 105078.

KATZ Ilan, et al., 2022. "One Year into COVID-19: What Have We Learned about Child Maltreatment Reports and Child Protective Service Responses?" *Child Abuse & Neglect* 130: 105473.

LYNEHAM Samantha and FACCHINI Lachlan, 2019. "Benevolent Harm: Orphanages, Voluntourism and Child Sexual Exploitation in South-East Asia." *Trends and Issues in Crime and Criminal Justice* 574: 1–16.

MATHEWS Ben, PACELLA Rosana, DUNNE Michael P., SIMUNOVIC Marko and MARSTON Cicely, "Improving measurement of child abuse and neglect: A systematic review and analysis of national prevalence studies." *PLoS one* 15, no. 1 (2020): e0227884.

MEZMUR Benyam Dawit, "The African Children's Charter@ 30: A distinction without a difference?" *The International Journal of Children's Rights* 28, no. 4 (2020): 693-714.

MOYO J., 2021. "Children at heightened risk of abuse in Zimbabwe." https://www.a a.com.tr/en/africa/-children-at-heightened-risk-of-abuse-in-zimbabwe-/2432060

NHAPI Tatenda, "Zimbabwe's National Case Management System for child protection and enhanced rights realization for children with disabilities (CWDS)." *African Journal of Social Work* 10, no. 2 (2020): 124-131.

O'CONNOR R. BETANCOURT T.S. and NGOZI V. Enelamah, "Safeguarding the lives of children affected by Boko Haram: Application of the SAFE Model of Child Protection to a Rights-Based Situation Analysis." *Health and Human Rights Journal.* 23(1), 27-41, (2021, 1).

OKYERE Christiana, ALDERSEY Heather Michelle, LYSAGHT Rosemary and SULAIMAN Surajo Kamilu, "Implementation of inclusive education for children with intellectual and developmental disabilities in African countries: A scoping review." *Disability and Rehabilitation* 41, no. 21 (2019): 2578-2595.

OLAYIWOLA Peter, "Challenging stories about child domestic work: evidence from South-West Nigeria." *Third World Quarterly* 42, no. 11 (2021): 2690-2705.

OLOWU 'Dejo, "Protecting children's rights in Africa: a critique of the African Charter on the Rights and Welfare of the Child." *Int'l J. Child. Rts.* 10 (2002): 127.

PATEL Shilpa N., SHANMUGAM Indhu, OBONG'O Christopher, Zivai, KASESE MUPAMBIREYI Constance, BANGANI Zwashe and MILLER Kim S., "Child disciplinary practices, abuse, and neglect: Findings from a formative study in Chitungwiza, Zimbabwe." *Child Abuse & Neglect* 115 (2021).

PETERSON C., FLORENCE C. and KLEVENS J., 2015. "The economic burden of child maltreatment in the United States." *Child Abuse Negl.*

PETROWSKI Nicole, CAPPA Claudia, PEREIRA Andrea, MASON Helen and AZNAR DABAN Rocio, "Violence against children during COVID-19:

Assessing and understanding change in use of helplines." *Child Abuse & Neglect* 116 (2021).

RINGSON John and CHERENI Admire, "Efficacy of the extended family system in supporting orphans and vulnerable children in Zimbabwe: An indigenous knowledge perspective." *African Journal of Social Work* 10, no. 1 (2020): 99-108.

RUSSELL Douglas, HIGGINS Daryl and POSSO Alberto, 2020. "Preventing child sexual abuse: A systematic review of interventions and their efficacy in developing countries." *Child Abuse & Neglect* 102.

SAVE THE CHILDREN, 2023. "New research reveals ongoing violence and abuse of Palestinian children detained by Israeli Military." https://www.savethechildren.net/news/stripped-beaten-and-blindfolded-new-research-reveals-ongoing-violence-and-abuse-palestinian

SKOP Y., "Nearly Half of Israel's Children Suffer Physical, Sexual or Emotional Abuse, Study Finds." https://www.haaretz.com/2013-11-13/ty-article/.premium/half-of-israeli-children-suffer-abuse/0000017f-dbf0-df9c-a17f-fff8163e0000

SLOTH-NIELSEN Julia, "The African charter on the rights and welfare of the child." *Child Law in South Africa. 2nd edition. Claremont: Juta* (2017): 431.

SOLEHATI T., PRAMUKTI I., HERMAYANTI Y., KOKASASIH C.E. and MEDIANI H.S., "Current of child sexual abuse in Asia: A systematic review of prevalence, impact, age of first exposure, perpetrators, and place of the offense." *The Challenges and Opportunities for Nurses in the New Era Adaptation.* 9(T6), 2021.

STATISTA RESEARCH DEPARTMENT, 2023. "Child abuse in the U.S. total number of victims 2012-2021". https://www.statista.com/statistics/639375/number-of-child-abuse-cases-in-the-us/

THE LANCET, "Child maltreatment in Europe: taking a public health approach. *Editorial,* 382(9898).

TIEKU Thomas Kwasi, 2019. "The African Union: successes and failures." In *Oxford Research Encyclopedia of Politics*.

UNICEF. 2015. "Child Maltreatment in Asia-Pacific is costing countries US $209 billion each year, says UNICEF. 2015. https://www.unicef.cn/en/press-releases/child-maltreatment-asia-pacific-costing-countries-us-209-billion-each-year-says-unicef

VELEMÍNSKÝ SR Miloš, et al., 2020.. "Prevalence of adverse childhood experiences (ACE) in the Czech Republic." *Child Abuse & Neglect* 102.

WALKER Judith-Ann, "Early marriage in Africa-trends, harmful effects and interventions." *African Journal of Reproductive Health* 16, no. 2 (2012): 231-240.

DOMUNI-PRESS
publishing house of DOMUNI Universitas

« Le livre grandit avec le lecteur »
"The book grows with the reader."

Domuni Universitas

Domuni Universitas was founded in 1999 by French Dominicans. It offers Bachelor, Master and Doctorate degrees by distance learning, as well as "à la carte" (stand-alone) courses and certificates in philosophy, theology, religious sciences, and social sciences. It welcomes several thousand students on its teaching platform, which operates in five languages: French, English, Spanish, Italian, and Arabic. The platform is accompanied by more than three hundred professors and tutors. Anchored in the Order of Preachers, Domuni Universitas benefits from its centuries-old tradition of study and research. Innovative in many ways, Domuni consists of an international network that offers courses to students worldwide.

To find out more about Domuni:

www.domuni.eu

The Publishing House

Domuni-Press disseminates research and publishes works in the academic fields of interest of Domuni Universitas: theology, philosophy, spirituality, history, religions, law and social sciences. Domuni-Press is part of a lively research community located at the heart of the Dominican network. Domuni-Press aims to bring readers closer to their texts by making it possible, via the help of today's digital technology, to have immediate access to them, while ensuring a quality paperback edition. Each work is published in both forms. The key word is simplicity. The subjects are approached with a clear editorial line: academic quality, accessible to all, with the aim of spreading the richness of Christian thought. Six collections are available: theology, philosophy, spirituality, Bible, history, law and social sciences. Domuni-Press has its own online bookshop: www.domunipress.fr. Its books are also available on its main distance selling website: Amazon, Fnac.com, and in more than 900 bookshops and sales outlets around the world.

To find out more about the publishing house:

www.domunipress.fr

EXTRACT FROM THE CATALOGUE

Jean-François ARNOUX,
Et le désert refleurira.

Sabine GINALHAC,
Désir d'enfant. L'éclairage inattendu des récits bibliques.

Pierrette FUZAT,
Un nom au bout de la nuit. Le combat de Jacob.

Patrice SABATER,
La terre en Palestine/Israël.

Marie MONNET,
Emmanuel Levinas. La relation à l'autre.

Apollinaire KIVYAMUNDA,
Maurice Zundel, une biographie spirituelle.

Juliette BORDES,
Viens Colombe. Saint Jean de la Croix.

Joseph MARTY,
Christianisme et Cinéma.

Michel VAN AERDE,
Le père retrouvé

Monique-Lise COHEN, Marie-Thérèse DESOUCHE,
Emmanuel Levinas et la pensée de l'infini.

Claire REGGIO,
Le christianisme des premiers siècles.

Ameer JAJE,
Diaconesses. Les femmes dans l'Église syriaque.

Jean-Paul COUJOU (sous la direction de),
L'État et le pouvoir.

Françoise DUBOST,
L'Évangile des animaux.

Markus JOST,
La Bible à l'école d'Ignace de Loyola et de Menno Simons.

Paul TAVARDON, ocso,
  Trappistes en terre sainte. Des moines au cœur de la géopolitique. Latroun, 1890-1946 (T.1).

Paul TAVARDON, ocso,
  Trappistes en terre sainte. Des moines au cœur de la géopolitique. Latroun, 1946-1991 (T.2).

Marie MONNET (sous la direction de),
  La source théologique du droit.

Nilson Léal DE SA,
  La vie fraternelle.

Apollinaire KIVYAMUNDA,
  Maurice Zundel. La relation à Dieu.

Lara LOYE,
  Fraternités.

Bernadette ESCAFFRE,
  Vocations. Quand Dieu appelle.

Raphaël HAAS,
  Pleine conscience. Bouddhisme et christianisme en dialogue.

Augustin WILIWOLI,
  Axel Honneth. Lutter pour la reconnaissance.

Louis FROUART,
  Pascal. Cœur, Corps, Esprit.

Emmanuel BOISSIEU,
  Platon. Une manière de vivre.

Emmanuel BOISSIEU,
  Kant. Une philosophie de la liberté.

Marie MONNET,
  Dieu migrant.

Thérèse HEBBELINCK,
  L'Église catholique et les juifs (T.1 et T.2).

Béatrice PAPASOGLOU,
  Qu'est-ce que l'homme ?

Augustin WILIWOLI SIBILONI op,
  Ce que les philosophes disent du vivre-ensemble.

François MENAGER,
Yves Bonnefoy, poète et philosophe.

Nicole AWAIS,
L'art d'enseigner le fait religieux.

Thérèse M. ANDREVON,
Une théologie à la frontière (T.1 et T2).

Michel VAN AERDE,
Venez vous reposer. Antidotes spirituels au burn-out.

Agnès GODEFROY,
Bien vieillir, dans les pas d'Abraham.

Olivier BELLEIL,
Résolution des conflits dans l'Église primitive.

Anton MILH op & Stephan VAN ERP,
Identité et visibilité. Conflits de générations chez les Dominicains.

Denis LABOURE,
Astrologie et religion au Moyen Âge.

Jorel FRANÇOIS,
Voltaire, philosophe de la religion.

Augustin WILIWOLI SIBILONI op,
La reconnaissance. Réparer les blessures.

Jean Baptiste ZEKE,
Loi naturelle et post-humanisme.

Emmanuel BOISSIEU,
Paul Ricœur. Un inconditionnel de l'amour.

Ameer JAJE,
Le chiisme. Clés historiques et théologiques.

Jean-René PEGGARY,
L'aube d'une pensée américaine. L'individu chez H. D. Thoreau.

Jean-François ARNOUX,
Comme un feu dévorant. Flammèches d'une lecture incarnée de la Bible.

Olivier BELLEIL,
L'autre dans l'islam coranique.

Sœur Agnès DE LA CROIX,
Miroir juif des évangiles.

Jean-Michel COSSE,
Au centre de l'âme.

Jean-Paul BALDAZZA,
Antoine. Un saint d'Orient et d'Occident.

Ameer JAJE,
Marie dans l'islam.

Olivier PERRU,
Le corps malade.

Jesmond MICALLEF,
Trinitarian Ontology.

Abel TOE,
Pauvreté et développement au Burkina Faso.

Jude Thaddeus MBI AKEM,
Le développement en Afrique.

Claude LICHTERT,
Lire la Bible ensemble.

Jorel FRANÇOIS,
Voltaire, philosophe contre le fanatisme.

Bruno CALLEBAUT,
Les Évangiles. Leurs origines, leurs exégèses.

Claude LICHTERT,
La parole pour sortir de soi. Dieu et les humains aujourd'hui : parcours biblique.

Heriberto CABRERA REYES,
Effondrement, apocalypse ou renaissance ? Théologie en temps de crise.

Patrick MONJOU,
Comment prêcher à la fin du Moyen Âge ? (T. 1 et T. 2).

Robert PLÉTY,
À la découverte du Rabbi de Nazareth (T. 1).

Robert PLÉTY,
À la rencontre du Rabbi de Nazareth (T. 2).

Jules KATSURANA,
Guide pour la Prévention de la violence sexiste.

Jacques FOURNIER,
La Trinité, mystère d'amour.

Louis D'HÉROUVILLE,
Marie-Madeleine, femme pascale.

Olivier PERRU,
Martin-Stanislas Gillet (1875-1951). La peur de l'effort intellectuel.

Paul-Marcel LEMAIRE,
Vivre l'Évangile.

John Jack LYNCH,
Judith, Sarah and Esther. Jewish heroines.

Paul NYAGA,
Moral Consistency with Lonergan's Thought.

François FAURE,
Emmanuel Mounier : La personne est son engagement (T. 1).

François FAURE,
Emmanuel Mounier : Montrer, sans démontrer (T. 2).

Olivier-Thomas VENARD, Gregory TATUM,
Conversations sur Paul. « Supportez-vous les uns les autres ».

Isaac MUTELO,
Muslim Organisations in South Africa. Political Role Post-1948.

Stephen Musisi KASOZI,
Issues of Constitutionalism. A case study of Uganda.

Pierre Dalin DOMERSON,
La gestion des biens de l'Église. Enjeu Pastoral.

Philippe ANDRÈS,
Notre-Dame de Rocamadour. Du Moyen Âge à nos jours.

Oliver BARRETT,
Ecological Crisis. In Catholic Social Teaching.

Augustin WILIWOLI SIBILONI,
Négociation pacifique des conflits sociaux.

Alfred DIBAN KI,
Ubuntu et vie chrétienne.

Claude VALENTIN,
99 Questions sur l'Humanitaire.

Philippe MONTOISY,
Le chien militaire et la Première Guerre mondiale.

Alice NEPVEU-BARRIEUX,
La marine dans l'Ancien Testament. Représentations et enjeux.

Marie MONNET,
En chemin.

Christophe-Marie, O.P. MOGHA NGAMANAPO MUDAKA,
Quelle crise d'éducation ? Des slogans segmentés à l'hyperconscience de la liberté holistique.

Caroline FERRER,
Saint Jérôme. La représentation dans la collection Fesch en Corse.

Munguci D. ETRIGA,
Kwasi Wiredu. Thoughts. Conference proceeding from Tangaza University.

Isaac MUTELO,
Human Rights in Southern Africa. Theory and Practice.

Marc MITRI,
Le christ-médecin. La divinisation de l'homme comme guérison selon Grégoire de Nysse.

Manuel RIVERO,
Progresser dans la vérité. Père Marie-Joseph Lagrange, dominicain.

Bruno CALLEBAUT,
Les évangiles au carrefour des exégèses.

Michel VAN AERDE,
Domuni, une aventure collective. 1998 – 2023.

Didier PETERS,
La chaise et l'électron. Analyse de la pensée d'Alfred North Whitehead.

Augustin WILIWOLI,
Justice sociale : Nouveaux enjeux.

Claude VALENTIN,
   De Lascaux à l'intelligence artificielle. Histoire de la culture.

Michel VAN AERDE,
   Domuni, una aventura colectiva. 1998 – 2023.

Michel VAN AERDE,
   Domuni, a collective adventure. 1998 – 2023.

www.ingramcontent.com/pod-product-compliance
Lightning Source LLC
Chambersburg PA
CBHW071744270326
41928CB00013B/2795